D0196250

# THE MARRIAGE CHECKUP

Thank you for giving us the chance to look through this book.
*The Marriage Checkup* is an excellent workbook for marriage.
Dr. Wright's insights into communication and conflict resolution
are a great foundation for any relationship. We hope to build
off the things we learned for years to come.

### LUCAS AND CHRISTIE
#### MARRIED 8 MONTHS

What we enjoyed about *The Marriage Checkup* were the surveys.
We liked the idea of questions to read and answer individually and
then coming together to discuss the answers. It really made us think
about how we are—how we *really* are. It also helped us by bringing up
topics for discussion. We truly believe this book will bless all who
read it and apply its teaching with God's direction and guidance.

### ARGEN AND CHRISTINA
#### MARRIED 4 YEARS

We believe that every married couple, regardless of how long they have been married, should read and take *The Marriage Checkup*. This is our second marriage; I was married for 33 years when my first wife died from cancer. My present wife's husband also died from cancer, after 33 years of marriage. I thought this second marriage was a nearly perfect one; but after taking *The Marriage Checkup*, I found that there were some areas I needed to work on to make our marriage even better.

### MYLON AND JULIE
MARRIED 15 YEARS

After 17 years of marriage, we thought we knew pretty much everything there is to know about each other—but we were amazed to find areas to discuss! Chapter after chapter sparked great conversation and gave us the opportunity to rediscover our relationship. This book helped us identify areas that we needed to strengthen, and then gave us tools to address them. Through this incredible and easy-to-use resource, we deepened our compassion for each other and renewed our commitment to seeing God's best come to pass in our lives, both individually and as a couple.

### MARK AND CHRISTI
MARRIED 17 YEARS

*The Marriage Checkup* helped us locate the strengths in our relationship as well as the weaknesses. A great benefit was that it covered our spiritual relationship, which is foundational to sustaining a good marriage. We enjoyed learning that we have some major strengths to accompany the weaknesses!

### MIKE AND CHRIS
MARRIED 22 YEARS

# M*the*arriage
## CHECKUP

### DR. H. NORMAN WRIGHT

**Regal**

From Gospel Light
Ventura, California, U.S.A.

Published by Regal Books
From Gospel Light
Ventura, California, U.S.A.
Printed in the U.S.A.

Regal Books is a ministry of Gospel Light, an evangelical Christian publisher dedicated to serving the local church. We believe God's vision for Gospel Light is to provide church leaders with biblical, user-friendly materials that will help them evangelize, disciple and minister to children, youth and families.

It is our prayer that this Regal book will help you discover biblical truth for your own life and help you meet the needs of others. May God richly bless you.

*For a free catalog of resources from Regal Books/Gospel Light, please call your Christian supplier or contact us at 1-800-4-GOSPEL or www.regalbooks.com.*

All Scripture quotations, unless otherwise indicated, are taken from the *Holy Bible, New International Version®*. Copyright © 1973, 1978, 1984 by International Bible Society. Used by permission of Zondervan Publishing House. All rights reserved.

Other versions used are
AMP—Scripture taken from THE AMPLIFIED BIBLE, Old Testament copyright © 1965, 1987 by the Zondervan Corporation. The Amplified New Testament copyright © 1958, 1987 by The Lockman Foundation. Used by permission.
KJV—*King James Version*. Authorized King James Version.
THE MESSAGE—Scripture taken from *THE MESSAGE*. Copyright © by Eugene H. Peterson, 1993, 1994, 1995 . Used by permission of NavPress Publishing Group.
NASB—Scripture taken from the *New American Standard Bible,* © 1960, 1962, 1963, 1968, 1971, 1972, 1973, 1975, 1977 by The Lockman Foundation. Used by permission.
NCV—Scriptures quoted from *The Holy Bible, New Century Version,* copyright " 1987, 1988, 1991 by Word Publishing, Nashville, Tennessee. Used by permission.
TLB—Scripture quotations marked (*TLB*) are taken from *The Living Bible,* copyright © 1971. Used by permission of Tyndale House Publishers, Inc., Wheaton, IL 60189. All rights reserved.

© 2002 H. Norman Wright
All rights reserved.

Cover and interior design by Robert Williams
Edited by Amy Simpson

Library of Congress Cataloging-in-Publication Data

Wright, H. Norman.
    The marriage checkup / H. Norman Wright.
        p. cm.
Includes bibliographical references (p.            ).
    ISBN 0-8307-3069-9 (trade paper)
    1.  Marriage—Religious aspects—Christianity.     I.  Title.
    BV835 .W744 2002
    306.872—dc21                                                                2002006511

1   2   3   4   5   6   7   8   9   10   11   12   13   14   15   /   09   08   07   06   05   04   03   02

Rights for publishing this book in other languages are contracted by Gospel Light Worldwide, the international nonprofit ministry of Gospel Light. Gospel Light Worldwide also provides publishing and technical assistance to international publishers dedicated to producing Sunday School and Vacation Bible School curricula and books in the languages of the world. For additional information, visit www.gospellightworldwide.org; write to Gospel Light Worldwide, P.O. Box 3875, Ventura, CA 93006; or send an e-mail to info@gospellightworldwide.org.

# Contents

# Preface

## An Exceptional Marriage—Fact or Fiction?

We hear way too much about marriages that are in trouble or don't make it. Yet there are many, many couples today who have fulfilling marriages, even exceptional ones. It is no accident that the strong marriages are the way they are. Good marriages don't just happen. The couples in exceptional marriages are willing to learn and grow; develop a positive, biblical attitude; and discover how to speak their spouse's language and celebrate differences.

So does an absolute formula exist that couples today can follow to guarantee the marriage they want? You already know the answer to that question—no. But there are principles that have worked for many. Consider the information in this book as your own personal consultation with the nation's leading authorities on what makes marriages work. Do not rely on your own experiences and opinions or those of your parents or friends. In place of going to a weeklong marriage seminar or 20 counseling sessions, you can read and glean from this resource what you would hear in the seminar or session; however, don't expect numerous stories or clever examples. What you will find here is bottom line and to the point. But no matter where you learn, you still need to apply it willingly. What you learn works, but it's up to you to apply it. These principles and guidelines have made a difference for so many, and they can also work for you.

You see, your marriage is a lifelong adventure. Every journey has its highs, lows and detours. And every journey is unique. No two couples experience the same road. Many experience marriage without giving it much thought, while others constantly take their marital temperature. Some underrate marriage and only see the problems and what isn't there. Others view marriage with blinders on and are oblivious to issues that eat away at the core of marriage. Which of these descriptions do you connect with?

Think of it this way: Your marriage is like a car. Every now and then it needs a tune-up. Often when your car is receiving a tune-up, the mechanic may find the beginning of a problem and take corrective action. This minimizes the damage. However, if you neglect this service, something may break, resulting in a major overhaul. And that's more expensive, time-consuming and disruptive. It is the same when you assess your marriage. You may discover the seeds or new growth of a problem that was hidden like termites in the foundation of a house. Once discovered, you have a head start and can begin to take corrective action.

If you feel in any way that your marriage could benefit from some corrective action (and every relationship could use a boost, since we're all flawed), I encourage you to continue and self-evaluate such things like your satisfaction in your marriage, how well you and your spouse communicate and what love language you speak. Are you ready? Great—let's go!

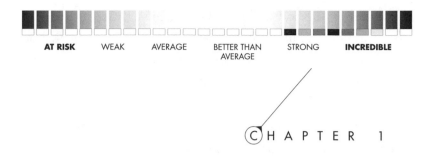

CHAPTER 1

# How Satisfying Is Your Marriage?

"Our marriage isn't perfect. There is no such animal—and that gives us encouragement. But our marriage is good. In fact, it's more than good. It's healthy, fulfilling, challenging, committed, fun and more than we thought it could ever be." Why can some couples make this statement? It isn't always like this. I have talked with many discouraged couples who ask, "Is this all that marriage can be? There's got to be more than this!" And there was more when they discovered how to build the marriage they wanted!

That is what I hope this book will do for you—help you build the marriage you have always wanted. Now I am sure you're thinking, *Well, Norm, that's good and all, but how?*

To answer the how question, I first need to address the purpose of this book. This book was designed to give you a snapshot of your marriage so that you, as an individual or as a couple, can determine the current state of your marriage. More important,

## Think of reading this book as the starting point for improving your marriage and taking it to new heights.

the information in this book can serve as the starting point to help you improve your marriage and take it to new heights.

## BENEFITS FROM THE BOOK

What makes this book differ from the hundreds of other marriage books lining the bookshelves is that it is an inventory— a quantitative and qualitative series of questions that will reveal to you and your spouse where your marriage currently stands and where it has the potential to go. Based on my inventory *The Marriage Checkup Questionnaire*, both the self-scored and the reflective-type questions enable you to find solutions to problems and can relieve you of paying a counselor or seminar fee for something you and the Lord can accomplish![1] Should you desire to learn even more about your spouse and your marriage at the conclusion of this book, be sure to find two copies of the questionnaire for both you and your spouse to fill out and then discuss. I guarantee you will not walk away from the questionnaire or this book without many areas in your marriage to praise God for and the discovery of other areas to improve.

In this chapter, you will gauge the current state of your marriage by rating your and your spouse's satisfaction levels. Once you have completed the level-of-satisfaction survey at the end of this section, think of the score you and your spouse receive as the assessment marker of your marriage. This will come in handy when you've completed the book, because you will be able to look back and see where your marriage was when you began reading and can then decide where you plan to take your marriage, based on your answers to the inventory questions throughout the book.

After you know how you perceive your marital satisfaction, you will take one more scored survey based on what I feel is the key to marriage—communication. Located in chapter 2, this quantitative survey will provide additional insight and will allow you to grasp the differences and similarities in the way you both communicate, possibly solving some major sources of conflict even before you work your way through the rest of the book.

After learning a great deal about how you and your spouse communicate, you will go on to discover many other important aspects of marriage in the remaining chapters. An abundance of inventory questions are woven throughout each chapter. The questions are mainly subjective, meaning that they are designed for personal reflection and discussion. Additionally, there are Take-Away Questions at the end of chapters 3-9, "Final Thoughts" and the epilogue, which will stimulate you to think about ways you can improve your marriage. When reflecting on and answering the questions throughout the book, please be sure to look back on your quantitative scores (chapters 1 and 2) from the satisfaction and communication surveys. These scores will help you better assess your marriage in comparison to where you want it to go.

Keep in mind that this book will cause you to think and evaluate your relationship in ways you've probably never considered before. Many of the questions require a written response, which will create a totally new perspective than if you just thought about your answers. Through writing, you will experience some confirmations as well as some surprises. As you complete the book's inventory, here are some thoughts you might discover:

1. Your marriage is where you thought it was.
2. Your marriage is in much better shape than you realized. You may have concentrated on the problems, rather than noticing the positives. This is the case in many marriages.
3. Some problems may need focused attention and work, and now you have some specific direction. You have the ability to do this yourself or with the assistance of a pastor or counselor.

First things first: Let's see what you perceive to be your level of satisfaction within your marriage. Please feel free to photocopy both the level-of-satisfaction survey (see below) and the level-of-communication survey (chapter 2) so that you and your spouse can take them separately and then compare your answers.

# CURRENT LEVEL OF SATISFACTION

Use an X to indicate your level of satisfaction, with 0 meaning no satisfaction, 5 average and 10 super, fantastic, the best. Use a circle to indicate what you think your spouse's level of satisfaction is at the present time.

1. Our daily personal involvement with each other
   0   1   2   3   4   5   6   7   8   9   10

2. Our affectionate, romantic interaction
   0   1   2   3   4   5   6   7   8   9   10

3. Our sexual relationship

    0  1  2  3  4  5  6  7  8  9  10

4. The frequency of our sexual contact

    0  1  2  3  4  5  6  7  8  9  10

5. My trust in my spouse

    0  1  2  3  4  5  6  7  8  9  10

6. My spouse's trust in me

    0  1  2  3  4  5  6  7  8  9  10

7. The depth of our communication together

    0  1  2  3  4  5  6  7  8  9  10

8. How well we speak one another's love language

    0  1  2  3  4  5  6  7  8  9  10

9. How we divide chores

    0  1  2  3  4  5  6  7  8  9  10

10. The way we make decisions

    0  1  2  3  4  5  6  7  8  9  10

11. How we manage conflict

    0  1  2  3  4  5  6  7  8  9  10

12. Adjustment to one another's differences

    0  1  2  3  4  5  6  7  8  9  10

13. Amount of free time spent together

    0  1  2  3  4  5  6  7  8  9  10

14. Quality of free time spent together
    0   1   2   3   4   5   6   7   8   9   10

15. Amount of free time spent apart
    0   1   2   3   4   5   6   7   8   9   10

16. Our interaction with friends as a couple
    0   1   2   3   4   5   6   7   8   9   10

17. The way we support each other in rough times
    0   1   2   3   4   5   6   7   8   9   10

18. How we support each other's careers
    0   1   2   3   4   5   6   7   8   9   10

19. Our spiritual interaction
    0   1   2   3   4   5   6   7   8   9   10

20. Our church involvement
    0   1   2   3   4   5   6   7   8   9   10

21. The level of our financial security
    0   1   2   3   4   5   6   7   8   9   10

22. How we manage money
    0   1   2   3   4   5   6   7   8   9   10

23. My spouse's relationship with my relatives
    0   1   2   3   4   5   6   7   8   9   10

24. My relationship with my spouse's relatives
    0   1   2   3   4   5   6   7   8   9   10

Scoring Key for Your Current Level of Satisfaction

To determine your score, add the numbers you made an X through for each statement. The sum reflects your score. To determine your spouse's score, add the numbers you circled for each statement. The sum reflects your spouse's score.

Your score _____

Your spouse's score _____

| | |
|---|---|
| 192-240 | Your relationship is doing very well. |
| 144-191 | Your relationship has some major strengths. |
| 121-143 | Your relationship reflects both strengths and weaknesses. (Any satisfaction level under 6 would benefit from some work.) |
| 73-120 | Definite improvement needed. |
| 72 and below | Major assistance needed as soon as possible. |

Select any three statements that have a satisfaction level of 3 or lower (or select your three lowest-scoring statements), and indicate what needs to occur for you to gain a higher level of satisfaction. List what you have tried or plan to try.

To obtain a visual picture of your marital satisfaction, draw a line the length of your marriage. Your line will start over the first year of marriage marker on the horizontal axis; your satisfaction at the time will determine where the line starts on the vertical axis—either low, medium or high. Your line should reveal a continuum from your satisfaction level when you first got married to your satisfaction level now. If you need to change the numbers at the bottom of the graph, please feel free to do so.

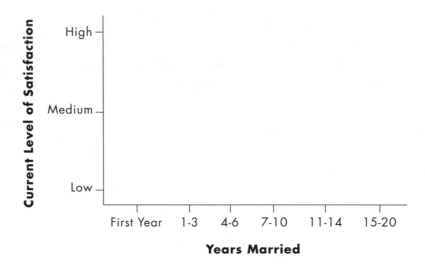

This concludes the first step in determining the current state of your marriage. You should now have a better sense of your marital satisfaction. And in order to obtain the most accurate picture of where you and your spouse are, please continue on to step two—determining your level of communication.

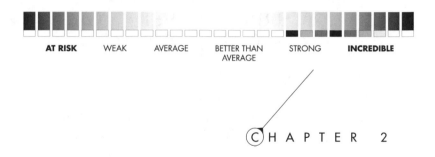

AT RISK    WEAK    AVERAGE    BETTER THAN    STRONG    **INCREDIBLE**
                              AVERAGE

## CHAPTER 2

# How Do We Communicate?

Now that you have a better sense of your marital satisfaction, it is time to determine your and your spouse's current communication level. The reason I picked communication over other marital aspects for the second and final quantitative survey is because there is usually high to moderate correlation between your satisfaction and your communication levels. Therefore, the communication-level scores (along with the satisfaction-level score) will give you a more accurate snapshot of your marriage relationship.

# CURRENT LEVEL OF COMMUNICATION

Use an X to indicate your level of communication, with 1 meaning almost never, 2 meaning rarely, 3 meaning sometimes, 4 meaning often and 5 meaning almost always. Use a circle to indicate what you think your spouse's level of communication is at the present time.

1. Listens when the other person is talking

    1     2     3     4     5

2. Appears to understand spouse when he or she shares

    1     2     3     4     5

3. Tends to amplify and say too much

    1     2     3     4     5

4. Tends to condense and say too little

    1     2     3     4     5

5. Tends to keep feelings to oneself

    1     2     3     4     5

6. Tends to be critical or nag

    1     2     3     4     5

7. Encourages spouse

    1     2     3     4     5

8. Tends to withdraw when confronted

    1     2     3     4     5

9. Holds in hurts and becomes resentful
   1      2      3      4      5

10. Lets spouse have say without interrupting
    1      2      3      4      5

11. Remains silent for long periods of time when the other is angry
    1      2      3      4      5

12. Fears expressing disagreement if the other becomes angry
    1      2      3      4      5

13. Expresses appreciation for what is done most of the time
    1      2      3      4      5

14. Complains that the other person doesn't understand him or her
    1      2      3      4      5

15. Can disagree without losing his or her temper
    1      2      3      4      5

16. Tends to monopolize the conversation
    1      2      3      4      5

17. Feels free to discuss sex openly with spouse
    1      2      3      4      5

18. Gives compliments and says nice comments to spouse
    1      2      3      4      5

19. Feels misunderstood by spouse
    1      2      3      4      5

20. Tends to avoid discussions of feelings

    1      2      3      4      5

21. Avoids discussing topics or issues that are problems

    1      2      3      4      5

**Scoring Key for Your Current Level of Communication**
*Statements 1,2,7,10,13,15,17 and 18*
To determine your score, add the numbers you make an X through for each of these eight statements. The sum reflects your score. To determine your spouse's score, add the numbers you circled for each of these eight statements. The sum reflects your spouse's score.

Your score _____
Your spouse's score _____

    33-40    You're doing very well.
    25-32    You're doing well.
    17-24    Some areas need improvement.
    9-16     Definite improvement needed.
    0-8      The relationship needs major assistance.

Any statements having a communication level of 3 or lower would benefit from some work. Any statements with a level of 1 may need outside assistance.

*Statements 3,4,5,6,8,9,11,12,14,16,19,20 and 21*
To determine your score, add the numbers you make an X through for each of these 13 statements. The sum reflects your score. To determine your spouse's score, add the numbers you circled for each of these 13 statements. The sum reflects your spouse's score.

Your score _____
Your spouse's score _____

| | |
|---|---|
| 53-65 | The relationship needs major assistance. |
| 40-52 | Definite improvement needed. |
| 27-39 | Some areas need improvement. |
| 14-26 | You're doing well. |
| 8-13 | You're doing very well. |

Any statements having a communication level of 3 or higher would benefit from some work. Any statements with a level of 5 may need outside assistance.

**Sharing Responses**
Make a date to share your responses with your spouse. Be sure to follow these positive communication guidelines when sharing responses:

1. Set a time and select a place where there are no interruptions from people, phones, etc.
2. Hold your spouse's hand (this helps keep a lid on emotions).
3. Begin by sharing how you scored yourself. If any statement in the first set had a level of 3 or lower, or if any statement in the second set had a score of 3 or higher, state your intentions for improving this area.
4. After you've both shared your scores, continue to hold your spouse's hand and share the scores that reflect how you see one another. Don't say "You do this" or "You don't do this" but, rather, "This is my perspective" or "This is the way I see the situation."

For any statement in the first set with a level of 3 or
lower, or for any statement in the second set with a
level of 3 or higher, say, "Here is something I'd like
you to think about" or "I would really appreciate it if
you would work on this."

5. When your spouse shares how he or she sees you and
makes a request, do not be defensive, point out an
exception or blame the other. Just say, "Thank you
for sharing your perspective. I'd like to think about
that." You're not agreeing with your spouse or admit-
ting he or she is correct. You're just considering his
or her view.

Now that you have determined your marriage satisfaction
and communication levels, go back and reflect on your scores.
Feel free to think about or journal about where you feel your
marriage currently stands.

Now what? I am a firm believer that communication can
either inhibit or promote relational success. So let's go ahead
and address one of the most important marital aspects right
from the start—communication. Learning the differences in how
people communicate will serve as a stepping-stone from the
quantitative part of the book to the qualitative part. While chapters 1 and 2 focused on the quantitative results (or where your
marriage relationship currently stands), the remaining chapters
focus on the subjective results (or where you want your marriage
relationship to go). What you should strive for throughout the
rest of the book is to bridge the gap between where your marriage currently stands and where you want it to go. As you
continue to read this book, think to yourself, *How can I get from
point A to point B?*

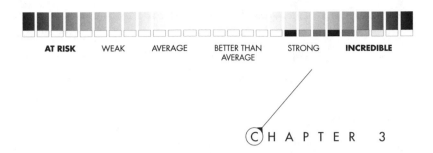

ⒸH A P T E R    3

# Love Comes in a Package

How are you at packaging and presenting your love to your spouse? To put it simply, how well do you communicate? What love language do you speak? I ask these questions because so many individuals don't feel loved or communicated with by their spouse. Yet, when I talk with their spouse, the story is just the opposite. They do love and feel connected to their spouse, but they are frustrated. They feel as if their efforts are either not registering or are not appreciated by their spouse. In time, the frustrated person may give up.

If you or your spouse is feeling like this, it is alright. There is a solution, and it is simple: you need to repackage the way you communicate so that your communication connects with your spouse.

You may communicate or share your love in the way you would like to be loved and communicated with, but it may not be the way your spouse prefers. You have to adapt to your spouse's preference. Everyone has a preferred language of receiving love. If you speak their language, your spouse hears it. Think of each love language as a different foreign language. If everyone around you speaks a different language, you probably will understand little to none of the conversations. It will sound like gibberish to you. But if those around you switch to your native tongue, you will understand. The same concept applies to the love languages.

Stu Weber elaborates on this concept in his book *Tender Warrior*:

I'm reminded of a cross-cultural snapshot one of my friends described to me. On a brief trip to Haiti, he found himself alone in a room with a young Haitian man who seemed wide-eyed with excitement about meeting an American. The Haitian obviously longed to open a conversation. His hands opened and closed. His eyes burned with a desire to weave his thoughts into understandable words. He seemed to have a thousand questions on the tip of his tongue. But my friend didn't speak a word of Creole and the Haitian didn't speak English. So eventually, after a few smiles, nods, vague gestures and self-conscious shrugs, the two young men strolled awkwardly to different corners of the room, and they parted—almost certainly for the rest of their lives.

That little experience paints a powerful analogy in my mind. You and I know men and women who live together ten, twenty, *fifty* years or more but never learn to speak one another's language. They sit in rooms together, ride in cars together, eat meals together, take vacations together and sleep together when the sun goes down. But for year after empty year they never learn how to get beyond vague gestures and a few surface phrases.[1]

And it is true that many couples speak a language that is different in structure, style and meaning, which can result in "crossed wires," or mixed messages.

> **Many couples speak a language that is different in structure, style and meaning, which can result in "crossed wires," or mixed messages.**

Don't worry though. This is not a fatal condition. It is just a matter of "rewiring," or learning about your spouse's love language. This can make the difference between marital health and marital anguish. Seldom do a husband and wife have the same love language, but they can learn a new one. Remember, you can't rely on your native tongue if your spouse doesn't speak the same language.

Speaking your spouse's language is not limited to vocabulary. It includes what I call an individual's packaging. For example, packaging refers to whether a person is an expander (sharing great volumes of detail) or a condenser (sharing little more than the bottom line). If your spouse is an expander, in addition to his or her seeing, hearing or feeling preferences, he or she most likely gives a lot of information and detail. If your spouse is a condenser, he or she probably keeps it brief. This is just one way we as individuals communicate differently with our spouses. Read on to find out more about your and your spouse's communication styles.

# YOUR LOVE LANGUAGE

The five love languages you may already be familiar with are from Dr. Gary Chapman's book *The Five Love Languages*:

1. *Words of Affirmation*—saying "I love you"; sincerely admiring, praising or complimenting your spouse; encouraging him or her and expressing your positive feelings in words—these are all ways to use words that affirm.
2. *Acts of Service*—doing nice things for the other and helping out are acts of service. Serving the other says, "I care enough for you to go out of my way to spend my time to help you."
3. *Gifts*—buying a gift or making a gift for the other says, "I was thinking of you and I was willing to put my thoughts into action by getting something for you." The gift might be small or large.
4. *Physical Touch or Closeness*—touching, patting, rubbing, head rubs, back rubs, foot tickles and sexual caresses are all examples of physical touch or closeness. Being near the other, bumping up against the other and putting an arm around the other are other examples.
5. *Quality Time*—hanging out together, spending exclusive time together and talking about things that are important to each of you show that you care for each other through conversation.[2]

Most people develop their pattern of love language based on a particular learning style. We learn in several ways, but most of us have a preference, which in turn usually determines the "languages" we speak.

Both you and your spouse have a dominant sense through which you prefer to receive communication (i.e., your learning style). We all see, hear and feel—the three dominant senses. One of your primary missions as a husband or wife is to discover your spouse's dominant sense and center your communication in that area. Gregory Popcak highlights the fact that it is important to be aware of different love languages in order to avoid miscommunication:

Differences between love languages are remarkable. Having a different primary love language than your spouse can lead to a great deal of miscommunication. The main reason for this is that people who are masters of one love language tend to disregard or devalue the others because they literally don't make "sense" to them. For example, if you have a primarily auditory love language, you may say, "I love you" many times per day to your more visual mate, and while this is very meaningful to you, he will probably be thinking, "It's easy for her to *say* how much she loves me, but I wonder why she never does anything to *show* me." Conversely, your more visual mate may write you notes, give you cards, and be very conscious of creating a romantic atmosphere, but as much as you appreciate these things, you may be suspicious of him because "He doesn't ever *tell* me how he feels" (visual people tend to live in their heads).

Kinesthetic spouses tend to be very physical. They literally need to "be in touch" with their spouses to "feel

connected." They can never get enough touching, holding, hugging, kissing, cuddling, or lovemaking. They
do, however, max out fairly quickly on conversation
(evidenced by the glazed look they get in the presence of
highly auditory people) and don't tend to appreciate many
visual romantic gestures (cards, flowers, pretty wrapping
paper) because they are simply not functional. People who
have a primarily kinesthetic love language tend to love
quiet times together, just sitting, being, and holding.[3]

Learn to speak the love language of your spouse, instead of insist-
ing that he or she adapt to your love language. As you learn to
communicate in your spouse's language, you'll experience a great
improvement in your relationship!

Let's investigate each of the three senses more closely to find
out how to communicate in specific love languages. The following
material is based on the studies of multiple therapists.[4]

**The Visual Person**
The visual person (whether male or female) relates to the world
around him in terms of how things look to him. When he imag-
ines, he visualizes; and when he remembers, he recalls a picture. He
experiences life through his eyes. He is primarily a watcher of
movies, TV, sporting events, people, art exhibits, museums or
scenery. He probably prefers reading, collecting items to look at,
taking pictures and looking at you. He is often concerned with how
he looks to others. A visual person talks about how things look,
rather than how he feels. Often a visual person tends to withdraw
and brood when upset, rather than talking through the problem.

A visual person prefers face-to-face conversations over the
telephone and responds well to written messages. He wants to
see a letter firsthand, rather than have it read to him. A visual

person who travels wants a map nearby and prefers to study it himself, rather than have it read to him.

Convey your love to a visual person by giving him something he can see—a picture, an object, a love note, etc. He may be concerned with the way he looks to you and especially the way you look to him.

How can you tell if a person is visually oriented? Listen to the words he uses. Here is a list of statements that are more typical of a visual person:

- From my point of *view* it *looks* this way.
- I *see* what you're driving at.
- That *looks* like a sure thing.
- That's really *clear* to me.
- What you're *picturing* is this or that.
- I don't know; I've *drawn a blank.*
- *Show* me what you're getting at.
- There's a *clear pattern* to this.
- It's beginning to *dawn* on me.

If you are an astute spouse, you will listen to the language of your spouse and begin to respond in like manner.

Here are some statements you can use in response to the visual person:

- I'm beginning to *see* your point of *view.*
- That *looks* good to me.
- What you shared with me really *lights* up my day.
- You know, I can just *picture* us on the beach in Maui.

Practice using visually oriented words, especially if they are new to you. Write down a list of visual words—as many as possible—and look for ways to use them in conversation with your visually oriented spouse. If you usually say, "That *feels* good to me," change it to, "That *looks* good to me." You may feel awkward at first as you try out a new vocabulary. Continue to practice and you will soon feel at ease.

Don't expect your spouse to notice your change in vocabulary. He or she probably won't be consciously aware of a language improvement. But your visual spouse will feel more comfortable in relating to you, perhaps without even knowing why.

Men tend to be more visual than women; in fact, most men are visual people. Women tend to lean toward feelings. But both men and women can learn to strengthen the two senses that are subordinate to their dominant language. Over the years, the visual trait has been and still is my strong suit. However, I have worked on the other two senses, auditory and feelings, and now enjoy a greater balance.

If you live with a visual person, you must adjust to his dominant style of perception. For example, if you are planning to buy new chairs for the family room, you will want to discuss how the room's appearance will improve in addition to how comfortable the chairs will be. If you want to escape to a quiet retreat with no phones and few people, emphasize to your visual spouse the scenic aspects of the location. And for the sexual dimensions of marriage, there are special applications of lovemaking to which the visual spouse is more inclined.

### The Auditory Person

The auditory person (whether male or female) is interested in hearing about life. This spouse relates more to sounds than sights. When the auditory person reads, she doesn't see pictures but hears words. If your spouse is auditory, don't expect her to notice a new article of clothing, hairdo, room arrangement or plant in the yard. You need to tell her more than you show her. She prefers talking about something to looking at it. Long conversations are important to the auditory spouse, and she tends to remember what she hears better than others.

If you want to share feelings, the auditory spouse will best understand the feelings if you verbalize them. She hears equally what is said and not said, and she is astute at picking up tonal changes and voice inflections. Harsh responses may be upsetting to her. The telephone is an important part of her life.

Auditory people fall into two different categories. Some feel compelled to fill the silent moments of life with sound: talking, playing the stereo, humming, etc. But others prefer quiet. Why would an auditory person opt for silence? Because many of them are carrying on internal conversations and external sounds cause interruption. Sometimes a silent auditory person's spoken responses may not make sense to you, because she fails to relate the full conversation occurring in her head aloud to you.

Romancing an auditory spouse must include saying "I love you" again and again. And since her hearing sense is so acute, how you say it is as important as how often you say it. Discover the words, phrases and tones that best convey your spoken love and use them often.

Romancing your hearing-oriented spouse also means suggesting activities that she would especially enjoy. Here is a list of possible preferences:

- Enjoying outdoor sounds
- Talking, arguing, giving advice
- Listening to the radio, music, concerts
- Playing a musical instrument
- Attending lectures, giving lectures, teaching
- Operating a CB or ham radio

• Recording, writing or creating dialogs
• Using the telephone

Here are some of the statements an auditory person uses:

• That *sounds* good to me.
• Let's *talk* about this again.
• Boy, that's *music* to my *ears.*
• People seem to *tune* him out when he is talking.
• *Harmony* is important to me.
• I *hear* you clear as a *bell.*
• *Tell* me a little more about it.
• Give me a *call,* so we can discuss the proposal.
• Your *tone* of voice is coming through *loud* and *clear.*

What kinds of responses should you use with an auditory person? Use words and phrases that focus on sound. Identify the words, write them down and practice them. A simple change from "Doesn't that *look* good to you?" to "Doesn't that *sound* good to you?" will make a difference to an auditory person. Instead of asking, "Would you like to go *see* that new movie with me?" ask, "How does attending that new movie *sound* to you?" Asking an auditory person to share her feelings may not provoke a response; but asking her to say what comes to mind when she hears the words "love," "romance" or "sexy" will tap into her auditory style. Now you're speaking her language.

**The Feelings Person**
Some people tend to be more feelings oriented, although it is more often true of women than men. Feeling people tend to touch a lot. They often desire to develop deep relationships. They crave closeness, love and affection. They are generally "right

brain" people, operating more intuitively than logically or analytically. Physical comfort and bodily sensations are important parts of their language style.

Feelings people often show their feelings but do not verbalize their feelings well. You can usually read happiness, sadness, anger, love or delight on their faces, or hear these emotions in the tone of their voices. And they are concerned about how others feel toward them. A feelings-oriented man who can effectively verbalize his emotions can be one of the easiest husbands to live with.

Feelings people are more spontaneous than auditory or visual people. This trait can be both positive and negative. On the one hand, they are free to create spur-of-the-moment, fun activities. On the other hand, for no apparent or logical reason, they might change their minds and upset the schedule of a plan-in-advance spouse.

Here are some statements often used by a feelings-oriented person. The word "feel" will be used in a variety of contexts.

- I have some good *vibes* about this.
- I have a *sense* about that.
- I like to get *close* to you.
- That person was so *sensitive*.
- I'm so *happy* today. Yesterday I was *unhappy*.
- I like being *near* you.

You will also hear words like "touch," "tense," "pressure," "hurt," "touchy," "soft," "smooth," "handle" and "relaxed" from a feelings person. Whereas the visual person says, "It *looks* good to me," and the auditory person says, "It *sounds* good to me," the feelings person says, "It *feels* good to me," "I'm *comfortable* with that" or "I understand how you *feel*."

Romance your feelings spouse by suggesting activities filled with personal experience, social contact and emotional stimulation. Involve other sensations such as taste and smell. In fact, many feelings people, especially men, really enjoy food. A special meal in a restaurant or dining room with just the right ambiance can be very romantic.

And finally, feelings people like to be known for their sensitivity. A wise spouse will notice this trait and comment on it often. Feelings people like to be touched often, especially when being spoken to.

### The Bottom Line

You may think, *Changing the way we talk to one another sounds like a pointless game that requires a lot of work.* Yes, it is work but not a game. Effective communication requires sensitizing yourself to and diligently accommodating the uniqueness of your spouse. By learning

## By learning new ways to talk, you and your spouse can climb out of communication ruts and become more flexible.

new ways to talk, you and your spouse can climb out of communication ruts and become more flexible. Changing your style of communication can make the difference between holding your spouse's attention and being ignored. This seems like reason enough!

## DIFFERENT MATCHUPS

What happens when two people with different perceptions marry? Let's consider some of the possible matchups and their results.

## The Visual and Auditory Couple

If a visual person marries an auditory person, the auditory spouse may not meet the visual spouse's standards for dressing, because the auditory person is less concerned about fashion. The visual person may favor neatness and orderliness in the household because of its visual attractiveness, but the auditory person might not care. The auditory person may forget the visible shopping list his or her spouse provides but will have better success remembering verbal lists and instructions.

What if the husband is visual and the wife is auditory? Let's look at a scenario. He attempts to *show* his love by buying her flowers and gifts and taking her places. Then one day she says, "You don't love me." He is floored. He points to all the things he has given her, but she simply says, "You never tell me you love me." To the auditory wife, words are more important than gifts. She would have preferred verbal words of affirmation, instead of visual keepsake objects.

The auditory wife may also err by limiting her love for her visually oriented husband to words. He may appreciate his wife *telling* him of her love, but he will really get the message when his brain receives certain visual stimuli. Her attention to grooming and dress, neatness in the home and pleasant sights, rather than sounds, will visually present her love.

Sometimes people come into my work area and rearrange my personal items. These people may think I don't notice, but I do. I have made some people uncomfortable when, in a home or a doctor's office, I take it upon myself to straighten a crooked picture on the wall. What does this say about me? I am more visually oriented.

## The Visual and Feelings Couple

Let's say a feelings man is married to a visual woman. He comes in the door and immediately grabs her, hugs her and cuddles her. She may pull away and say, "You're always grabbing me. All you want to do is touch. I want you to look at me, instead of sneaking up behind me!"

Conversely, she needs to learn to talk to her husband through his feelings vocabulary. He needs touching, caressing and closeness to feel loved. He likes things to fit and be comfortable more than visually attractive. He wears an old shirt and a floppy hat that look awful to her but feel good to him. She must make room in her life for her husband's comfort need.

Showing how a couple clashes over buying new furniture is always a good example for this combination. The visual person wants the room to look neat and new while the feelings person wants to feel good and comfortable in the room. The loving solution? Agree on furniture that is both neat and comfortable, which meets the needs of both spouses.

The feelings person needs to respond to the visual spouse by talking about how he or she *sees* things. The visual spouse, in turn, should learn to develop a *feel* for those things that are important to his or her spouse. For example, here's a conversation between a feelings wife and a visual husband:

> *Marge*: John, I really would like a new outfit for the conference we're attending. I just don't have anything that feels comfortable. Nothing feels right anymore.
>
> *John*: But you seem to have several outfits in the closet that aren't very old and still look great. Why spend any more money?
>
> *Marge*: But I just don't feel good in them. Do you know what I mean?
>
> *John*: No, I don't. It appears to me you have lots of out-

fits that you don't wear that much. What's wrong with those?

*Marge (Beginning to see the light.)*: John, you're right. I do have a number of outfits. But none of them look very good on me. And for this conference I want to look my best for you. Why don't I bring home two or three outfits for you to see and we can go from there?

Guess what John said to that? There is a greater possibility that his response was affirmative because Marge was speaking his language.

Take a moment to see if you can identify which love language you prefer and which one your spouse prefers. List them in order of preference.

## GENDER DIFFERENCES

Before you move on to the love languages test provided in this chapter's Take-Away Questions section (which I hope will help you determine your and your spouse's languages), I feel there is one more area to broach that will help you better prepare for this test.

The second step in learning how to fully speak one another's love language is to understand the unique gender differences that exist between people. To learn more about these differences, including the myths and stereotypes, please read my book *Communication: Key to Your Marriage* in order to complete your marital language education. Once you've done this, your ability to relate better to your spouse, children and everyone will improve.

Consider the following monologue by a feelings wife expressing her concerns of being married to a visual husband. Keep in mind the idea that we as individuals hold strong personality traits based on our gender and sexual identity.

I wanted more nonsexual touching. After listening to the *Language of Love* presentation, I prayed, and God gave me a word picture to use with my husband.

Our marriage had gotten to the point where I didn't want my husband to touch me in any way. I'd curl up on my side of the bed and say "'Night." He would try to hold me and I'd turn away and find something I "had" to do. It was bad for both of us. I knew as a wife it was my duty to have sex, and so we did, but I'd roll over and cry afterwards. I did a lot of praying that God would change my feelings. I didn't want to hate his touch. I didn't hate him. We could talk easily about anything as long as we weren't touching.

God gave me a word picture. We are farmers and have an old diesel-run tractor. To start this tractor in the winter you have to push a button and hold it in to warm it up. Then it will start. I told him I was like this cold tractor. When he touched me in a sexual way, it was like turning the key on the tractor. It may sound like it would start—you may want it to start—but it won't; and as soon as you quit turning the key, it's over. But when you put your arm around me in church, hold my hand in the car, help me clear the table, kiss my neck and that's all, it's like holding in the little silver button and warming me up. Then when you "turn the key," I'll start! (He just cried. It was the first time he understood what I meant.) We agreed "no sex" for one month. I began not to feel threatened, and we began to enjoy each other's touch. It didn't happen overnight, but our marriage is stronger in all ways than ever before.

Our marriage is better than ever. Our sex life is better, but our nonsexual marriage is much better.

How do you feel after reading this? If you have ever felt this way, how do you think gender differences might have affected the situation?

Now after absorbing all this information, your first step is to learn one another's love language. Remember, your tendency will be to show love to your spouse in the way you want to be loved. Each of you needs to share with the other what your own love language is and then adapt. (If you are still having a difficult time discovering your and your spouse's love languages after the following test, please read *The Five Love Languages* by Gary Chapman.)

# TAKE-AWAY QUESTIONS

This section differs from the following chapters' Take-Away Questions in that it is a test, not a series of questions for personal reflection and discussion. The following test is based on what Tracy Cabot used in her book *How to Keep a Man in Love with You Forever*. The test will help you identify your and your spouse's love languages. The test will reveal whether you and your mate are seeing, hearing or feelings oriented. It is not foolproof, but it can help you and your spouse learn the love languages you speak, which will enhance communication.[5]

### Instructions

Read each question and then determine your answer. Place the letter that corresponds to your answer on the "Me" line. Then decide how your spouse would respond and place the letter that corresponds to his or her answer on the "My spouse" line.

1.  Given $1,000 to spend on one of the following, which would you choose?

    a. A new mattress
    b. A new stereo
    c. A new television

    Me _____ My spouse _____

2.  Which would you rather do?

    a. Stay home and eat a home-cooked meal
    b. Go out to a concert
    c. Go to a movie

    Me _____ My spouse _____

3.  Given a choice of activities at a resort, which would you choose?

    a. Going to a lecture
    b. Exploring hiking trails
    c. Relaxing and doing nothing

    Me _____ My spouse _____

4.  Which of these rooms would you most enjoy?

    a. One with a terrific view
    b. One with an ocean breeze
    c. One in a quiet corner

    Me _____ My spouse _____

5. To which event would you rather go?

    a. A wedding
    b. An art exhibit
    c. A party with friends

    Me _____ My spouse _____

6. Which are you considered?

    **a.** Athletic
    b. Intellectual
    c. Humanitarian

    Me _____ My spouse _____

7. How do you most often keep in touch?

    a. By talking on the phone
    b. By writing letters
    c. By having lunch

    Me _____ My spouse _____

8. How do you prefer to spend time?

    a. Talking
    b. Touching
    c. Looking

    Me _____ My spouse _____

9. If you lost your keys, what would you do?

    a. Look for them
    b. Shake your pocketbook or pockets to hear them jingle
    c. Feel around for them

    Me _____ My spouse _____

10. If you were going to be stranded on a desert island, what would you most want to take along?

    a. Some good books
    b. A portable radio
    c. Your sleeping bag

    Me _____ My spouse _____

11. Which type of dresser are you?

    a. Immaculate
    b. Casual
    c. Very casual

    Me _____ My spouse _____

12. Which of these would you rather be?

    a. In the know
    b  Very chic
    c. Comfortable

    Me _____ My spouse _____

13. If you had unlimited money, what would you do?

    a. Buy a great house and stay there
    b. Travel and see the world
    c. Join in the social scene

    Me _____ My spouse _____

14. If you could, which would you rather be?

    a. A great doctor
    b. A great musician
    c. A great painter

    Me _____ My spouse _____

15. Which do you think is sexiest

    a. Soft lighting
    b. Perfume
    c. Special music

    Me _____ My spouse _____

**Scoring**

First, translate your answers from the questions to the grid on next page. For example, if your answer to the first question is "a," this means you responded by feelings. Do this for all your responses by marking an X on the grid. Then on the grid do the same for your spouse, but use a circle to signify his or her response.

| 1. | a. feelings | b. auditory | c. visual |
|-----|-------------|-------------|-----------|
| 2. | a. feelings | b. auditory | c. visual |
| 3. | a. auditory | b. visual | c. feelings |
| 4. | a. visual | b. feelings | c. auditory |
| 5. | a. feelings | b. visual | c. auditory |
| 6. | a. visual | b. auditory | c. feelings |
| 7. | a. auditory | b. visual | c. feelings |
| 8. | a. auditory | b. feelings | c. visual |
| 9. | a. visual | b. auditory | c. feelings |
| 10. | a. visual | b. auditory | c. feelings |
| 11. | a. visual | b. auditory | c. feelings |
| 12. | a. auditory | b. visual | c. feelings |
| 13. | a. feelings | b. visual | c. auditory |
| 14. | a. feelings | b. auditory | c. visual |
| 15. | a. visual | b. feelings | c. auditory |

Second, count the number of your visual, auditory and feelings preferences by tallying the X marks. Then do the same for your spouse by tallying the circles. The category that captures the most answers suggests your and your spouse's primary love languages.

Myself:      Visual_____   Auditory_____   Feelings_____
My Spouse:  Visual_____   Auditory_____   Feelings_____

We have covered a lot of ground so far. By now you and your spouse should have determined your marital satisfaction and communication levels. Additionally, you and your spouse should have a better sense of which way each of you communicates love to the other. I encourage you at this point to again reflect and perhaps journal any thoughts, beliefs, praises or angst you see, hear or feel.

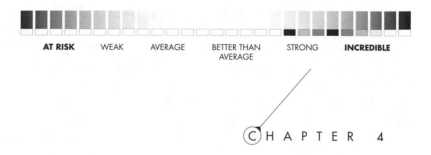

AT RISK   WEAK   AVERAGE   BETTER THAN   STRONG   **INCREDIBLE**
                          AVERAGE

# Marital Myths and Telling Truths

By now you should have a better sense (whether that be visual, auditory or feelings) of where your and your spouse's marriage currently stands. Were the satisfaction- and communication-level surveys helpful? I hope so. As we continue to move into other important aspects of marriage, there are a few long-held beliefs that need to be dispelled.

Two marriage researchers studied couples over a period of 20 years. Their findings may surprise you, as some of them counter beliefs many people have held for years. The beliefs disproved by the researchers are called conventional wisdom. I prefer calling them Marital Myths, or M & Ms.

# M & M:

## THE PERSON YOU MARRY HAS A GREAT DEAL TO DO WITH THE HAPPINESS YOU EXPERIENCE IN MARRIAGE

Actually, marital happiness depends little on the person you marry. Rather, it's how you cope with conflict (and I would add, how you handle one another's differences).

Years ago I found a statement that sums up this issue very well: At first we were concerned about meeting the "right one" to marry. Now we are learning how important it is to be the "right one" for someone else.[1]

If you treat the wrong person like the right person, you could have married the right person after all. On the other hand, if you treat the right person like the wrong person, you most likely married the wrong person. I also know that it is far more important to be the right person than it is to marry the right person. In short, whether you married the right or wrong person is primarily up to you. It is how you are treating that person that makes all the difference. That's something to think about!

Did you marry the wrong person? Maybe you did. You *certainly* did if your definition of the right person is someone who always understands you, inspires your passion, entertains you, reduces your loneliness, appreciates you, makes you feel good about yourself—in short, meets your expectations.

After an intense and disappointing disagreement with his wife, one husband expressed his frustration by saying, "Mary, you're not the woman I thought I married!" She looked at him with a slight smile and said, "I never was the woman you thought you married!"

Are any of us the people our spouses thought they married? Some individuals marry a phantom or a dream, and throughout their marriage they continue to chase that illusion. Many couples are surprised by marriage. Were you?

Regardless of why you married, the fact remains that you are married! Every couple encounters surprises in marriage. We can either allow the surprises to totally throw us, or we can use them as growth opportunities and make adjustments. Reality sets in once you are married, but don't think of it as being synonymous with trouble or disappointment! Instead, think of reality as the potential for making new discoveries and developing flexibility and protection against stagnation within a marriage relationship.

In some sense, we all choose a "wrong person" to marry, because there's something wrong with all of us. We are created in God's image, but at the same time, we are afflicted with the same fatal condition. The idea that we are born sinful has become politically incorrect, but the evidence is too strong to ignore. We are flawed. We are broken. We are all "wrong people."

You can understand this. It would be easy to label your spouse as the wrong person in your marriage. However, you've also been wrong when you contributed to any alienation in your relationship. You can continue to both work on the sin in your lives, in the hope that someday your marriage might get better and in the knowledge that, whatever the outcome, God can make you more caring and sensitive, more humble and prayerful. Work toward wholeness and holiness. It is a life and marriage changer.

# M & M:

### PERSONALITY FLAWS SUCH AS INSENSITIVITY OR INSECURITY ARE THE UNDERLYING CAUSES OF MARITAL DISTRESS (WE'RE NOT TALKING ABOUT CONTROL FREAKS, NARCISSISTS, BORDERLINES OR PSYCHOPATHS BUT THE EVERYDAY DEFECTS WE ALL COME WITH!)

Personality flaws don't predict marital happiness or stability. What's more important is how we respond to irritating behaviors.

# M & M:

## YOUR COMPATIBILITY OR SIMILARITY TO YOUR SPOUSE IS ONE OF THE MAIN REASONS THAT YOUR MARRIAGE SUCCEEDS

How similar or different you and your spouse are in personality does not affect the success of your marriage. Your success in marriage depends on how you handle your differences and similarities. Everyone marries a foreigner to some degree. You may have even married someone from the same cultural background or neighborhood, but the longer you're married, the more differences you discover in preferences, ways of doing things, how you talk, what you mean, etc. All of these can result in a major source of conflict or a major source of joy.

What is needed to make a marriage joyful and alive is to learn to celebrate your differences. That means you can look at one another and say, "It's alright for you to be you and for me to be me." Are you at that place yet? If not, there's hope.

One of the first steps in getting there is learning how to speak one another's language. When you understand and learn how to implement the differences you each bring to the marriage, your satisfaction and love level can climb. Misunderstanding that results from not knowing each other's differences begins to drop away like fleas off a shampooed dog. What love languages did you find out you and your spouse speak from the chapter 3 survey? Another important tool to use in understanding the communication differences you and your spouse bring into the marriage is my book *Communication: Key to Your Marriage*. You'll (and I mean both husband and wife) want to read this book, which explains the many differences couples face when relating to one another. Couples over the years have said, "If only we had known what is taught in that book years before, we would have avoided a lot of hurt and dissatisfaction in our marriage." The book is a basic outline of what I've taught (and had to learn myself) in seminars and counseling over the past 35 years. It is not just based on my thoughts but also on what I've learned from many others. Most important, it's based on Scripture, and I've shared it with anyone who would listen. The information provided in *Communication: Key to Your Marriage* does improve marriages! The content is totally different from what you'll find in this book. But one without the other leaves a gaping hole. Often it isn't the issue you're dealing with that's the problem—it's the communication packaging. So please read and apply the knowledge it contains. Both books will bring all the information together.

# M & M:

## PROBLEMS IN MARRIAGE WORK THEMSELVES OUT WITH TIME, SO LET THEM GO AND THEY'LL FIND THEIR OWN SOLUTION

Actually, problems get worse over time. They need to be tended to as soon as possible. The more ingrained the problem is, the more difficult it is to resolve. In time, a futile attitude replaces the sense of hope.[2]

# SIX TRUTHS OF RELATIONSHIP HAPPINESS

As you reflect on the marriage myths, which ones ring true for you? Any, all or perhaps none? If you find yourself believing some of the M & Ms, how do those beliefs impact your marriage? And what will you do now to change the negative effects?

Let's now move ahead and explore the six truths of relationship happiness. Take a moment to see if you can predict some of the truths. Write down your thoughts before proceeding.

### 1. Every Relationship Has a Hidden Reservoir of Hope

Even the worst marriage relationships have a seed of hope hidden somewhere in their depths. Have you ever considered that a destructive conflict or quarrel starts out with a hopeful intention? It's true. Even when a discussion gets away from where it started, remember that it started from the hope that change could be made. Have you ever said, "I wanted to share something with you for you to consider and reflect on. My reason for sharing is this" and stated your purpose? Too often we assume our spouse isn't going to listen, accept or like what is said, so it is either expressed defensively or in a critical attacking mode. No wonder the interchange doesn't go well and our hope changes into despair.

Have you ever considered during a disagreement that the statements you each make are actually said with the purpose of resolving the issue? One marriage specialist put it this way: "In the heat of conflict, statements might appear to others as though the partners were trying to pour gasoline on a fire already burning out of control, when in truth the speaker actually means for the statement to douse the fires of conflict."[3]

What can you do to make a difference? In your next disagreement or conflict, let your spouse know the intent of your comments. Also believe that your spouse's comments are also attempts to solve the problem. This is much better than assuming your spouse is purposely being destructive with a comment. Give him or her the benefit of the doubt. This will take a shift in your thinking process as well as your attitude. Remember, hope is a choice, and with hope you'll be amazed at some of the results.[4]

And since we're talking about conflict, let me throw in something else. Many conflicts between couples occur because of any one of the following:

- Each has a different thinking pattern or process that leads to conflict.
- Each has a different communication style that leads to conflict.
- Each has a lack of understanding and connection with the other.

Is this a major problem? No. It has a simple solution.

If one of you is an extrovert, you are energized by being with people. You talk first and think later. In fact, you need to talk to think. Sometimes you wish you could take back what you said. When it comes to disagreements or conflicts, extroverts believe if they can just say one more thing, it will solve the problem. Can you imagine the problem if both are extroverts?

If one of you is an introvert, you are drained by being with people too much and you get your energy from being alone. You need to think before you speak and often take six or seven seconds before responding. You won't say something unless you've thought it through, and you assume that others do the same. If someone (like an extrovert) pressures you, your mind may go blank or you'll say, "I need to think about that for a minute." In a disagreement, an extrovert may see you as withdrawing when you just need time to think first.

There is nothing wrong with being an extrovert or an introvert. This is just how God fashioned us. We're unique. But this uniqueness can become an irritant if there is no understanding. What can you do?

An introvert can say, "I'm not withdrawing. I want to think for a few seconds." You can also recognize the extrovert's greater need for being with people. Remember that an extrovert is talking out loud. They at times brainstorm aloud for everyone to hear. However, an extrovert doesn't always mean what they say when speaking out loud.

If you're an extrovert, recognize that your introvert spouse needs time alone to recharge. Let them know when you're just thinking out loud. Curb your tendency to make just one more comment in a disagreement. And when you ask your spouse a question, say, "Here's something I'd like you to think about," and give them time to think. Don't assume they're withdrawing when they're silent.

You'll be amazed at the difference this can make! Find out more about resolving conflict in your marriage with communication by reading *Communication: Key to Your Marriage*.

### 2. One Zinger Can Wipe Out 20 Acts of Kindness
Yes, it is true. You can have a wonderful day being kind, thoughtful and tender for hours, and then you open your mouth and

## A zinger has the power to render many positive acts meaningless.

share a put-down. It's as though a giant eraser came sweeping through your relationship and wiped out all your positive actions and words. This principle is similar to the fact that it takes 20 minutes of exercise to work off a candy bar but only one minute to eat another one and invalidate all the good effects of your exercise.

A zinger has the power to render many positive acts meaningless. Once a zinger has landed, the effect is similar to a radioactive cloud settling on an area of prime farmland. The land becomes so contaminated by radioactivity that even though seeds are scattered and plants are planted, they fail to take root. Subsequently, they die out or are washed away by the elements. It takes decades for the contamination to dissipate. After the expression of a zinger, kind acts and loving words find similarly hostile soil. It may take hours or days before new positive overtures are well received.[5]

Let's take a look at how merely rephrasing a complaint into a request can eliminate conflict. Very few people enjoy hearing complaints from their spouse. They feel judged, criticized, attacked, unaccepted and condemned. If that is the case, wouldn't it be better to eliminate all complaints, since they rarely work and do so much damage? No. The problem is not the complaints; many complaints are legitimate. It is the package they come in that produces conflict. It is possible to phrase a complaint in such a way that your spouse will not raise his or her defensive barriers. He or she will listen and consider what you are saying. Note the difference between a complaint and a request.

> *Complaint*—"I get so repulsed when you eat with your mouth open and then try to talk at the same time."
> *Request*—"I'd appreciate it if you would chew with your mouth closed. It does wonders for my response to you."

> *Complaint*—"This house looks like the place where the buffalo roam."

*Request*—"Let's talk about what can be done this week to clean and straighten up the house. I think we'd both feel better about it."

*Complaint*—"You're never affectionate anymore."
*Request*—"I would appreciate it if you could give me a kiss and a hug once a day."

*Complaint*—"You're so sloppy. I don't know why you don't listen to me. You're making me into your mother, you know."
*Request*—"It would help if you would take your dishes to the kitchen when you're through. Thanks for helping me in this way."

*Complaint*—"All you do is live for work, work, work. It's your mistress, and I resent it!"
*Request*—"I would like to spend a few minutes with you each day. Can we talk about how we can work that out?"

*Complaint*—"You're so inconsiderate and rude when you get on my case in front of the kids."
*Request*—"I'm upset when you criticize me in front of Tina and Mary. I'd like to hear what you have to say in private."

When you learn to edit your thoughts, consider the impact of your words and control what you say, your marriage handles bumps in the road much more easily. You see, the packaging, or how you present your words and actions, makes all the difference!

### 3. When You Make a Little Change, It Can Produce Major Changes in Your Relationship

It is true. When one person makes a change, the relationship can change. The problem is we usually think our relationship needs major changes, and it's our spouse who needs to make them. However, if you strongly feel your spouse needs to change, you need to create a climate for change.

Your request for change needs to be reasonable and attainable. In other words, is it something possible for your spouse to change? If you want to see a basic personality change, forget it. An extrovert will always be an extrovert, and an introvert will remain an introvert. But responses can be modified.

If you want a person's attitude to change, don't count on that happening. If you want your spouse to "feel what you feel" and with the same intensity, you're reaching for the impossible dream. However, you can ask for a change in behavior that can affect personality expression, attitudes and feelings. Your request should give you an affirmative response to the question, Will this request enhance our relationship and create a greater depth of intimacy? This is the fundamental purpose for change. The authors of *Two Friends in Love* give us some insightful guidelines:

> When change is needed in our traits and personalities, it is only in the realm of the man-inspired, man-prompted characteristics. Those that are God-given do not need touching up. They are fine the way they are. They only need to be acknowledged and appreciated. However, in the man-related realm, when there are characteristics that should be reworked because of the harmful effect they're having on the marriage, exercise great care in the way you handle change.[6]

To create a climate for change, you will need to be both persistent and patient. You'll need to keep trying in a creative, sensitive and loving manner, even when it doesn't seem to work. And you will need to be realistic and not expect too much. This is called patience.

## To create a climate for change, you will need to be both persistent and patient.

Will your request for change help your spouse as well as you? Will he or she become a stronger person? Will it increase Christian growth and maturity? Or is the request not that important after all? If you ask yourself these questions, you can become a skilled teacher, and both of you can assist each other in the growth process.

When I conduct premarital counseling, I ask a number of confrontational questions. In the initial session I ask, "What passage of Scripture would you like your fiancé to implement, which will make him or her an even stronger and more mature person?"

You can imagine some of the responses. About half of the individuals need a week to think about the answer. After they select a passage, I share my reason for the question. I tell them it's helpful to run a request for change through the grid of Scripture in order to see if God's Word has anything to say about it. (Even if Scripture is silent on the subject, the request may still be legitimate.) Consulting Scripture can help a person refine his or her requests for change.

For example, if we want our spouse to change something in their character, Galatians 5:22-23 reveals the ultimate model of qualities that we can encourage our spouse toward. We should desire the same qualities for ourselves!

> But the fruit of the [Holy] Spirit [the work which His presence within accomplishes] is love, joy (gladness), peace, patience (an even temper, forbearance), kindness, goodness (benevolence), faithfulness, gentleness (meekness, humility), self-control (self-restraint, continence). Against such things there is no law [that can bring a charge] (Gal. 5:22-23, *AMP*).

Remember that the message in your request is, "I care for you. My request is something I believe will benefit both of us, and it will mean so much to me. It's worth considering."

### 4. It Is Not the Differences Between Spouses That Cause Problems

It is how you deal with the problems that is important. When you learn new ways to respond to the problems, differences become strengths, not liabilities.

How do you feel about the fact that the two of you are so different? Is it a time of celebration or consternation? There is tremendous value in learning to appreciate your differences. Think about and write down five examples of how you and your spouse are similar and different.

In 1 Corinthians 12—14, we learn that diversity does not necessitate division. From these chapters, we can first learn to maximize the value of our differences. Second, we can learn that it is impossible to understand and appreciate who your spouse is without understanding his or her God-given uniqueness. Consider these thoughts from Kearsey and Bates' book *Please Understand Me*:

> If I do not want what you want, please try not to tell me that my want is wrong.
>
> If I believe differently than you, at least pause before you correct my view.
>
> If my emotion is less than yours, or more, given the same circumstance, try not to ask me to feel more strongly or weakly.
>
> If I act, or fail to act, in the manner of your design for action, let me be.
>
> I do not, for the moment at least, ask you to understand me. That will come only when you are willing to give up changing me into a copy of you.
>
> To put up with me is the first step to understanding me. Not that you embrace my ways as right for you, but that you are no longer irritated or disappointed with me for my seeming waywardness.
>
> In understanding me you might come to prize my differences from you, and, far from seeking to change me, preserve and even nurture those differences.[7]

Not only do we need to acknowledge our differences and be willing to value them, but more important, we also need to find a way to understand and make sense of those differences. And when you do, what a difference it makes in your marriage. Are you there yet, or is this an area needing work?

## 5. Men and Women Use Different Weapons When They're Upset, but These Lead to Similar Wounds

The authors of the book *We Can Work It Out* state, "Not only do men and women suffer similar wounds, they also sustain these wounds trying to accomplish the same objectives: acceptance, support and affection. When spouses try to understand what is not going right in a relationship, they tend to examine the current weapons that are being used rather than ultimate goals that are so strongly desired by both people."[8]

I've heard this so often in counseling when couples focus on what they don't like and what the other person did. They try to outdo one another with blame. No one hears. No one listens. Nothing changes until we ask, "What do you really want from your spouse?"

"I want to be loved."

"And what would make you feel loved?"

The typical answer to this question is key. Why? Because it tells you what your spouse needs for a fulfilling marriage. The best way to achieve fulfillment is through disarmament of the weapons or defensive barriers you use. Don't concentrate on these; rather, focus on what you want to accomplish. When positives become the focus, weapons are discarded. (For more information on conflict resolution, see chapter 12 of *Communication: Key to Your Marriage*.) Take a moment to respond to the following questions and see where your focus is:

1. What do you want to accomplish at this time?
2. What do you want from your spouse?

It also helps to know that the gender differences we discussed in chapter 3 come into play when resolving conflict. For example, men seem to have a harder time handling conflict, so they tend to withdraw. And if they're overwhelmed by their wife's talking, they tend to get angry, shut down the interaction and then withdraw.[9]

Women are often uncomfortable with emotional distance, so they prefer to resolve conflicts and do so immediately. Unfortunately, this can lead to the classic Pursuer-Distancer problem so often seen in marriages. For additional information in this area, read John Gray's books *Men Are from Mars, Women Are from Venus* and *Mars and Venus Together Forever*.

Let's consider a few positive steps to employ, which seem to work for most couples when dealing with conflicts and weapons.

## TRUCE TRIGGERS

Sometimes conflicts seem to consume a couple's time and attention. The couple spends their energy dwelling and ruminating about their times of conflict. Why not try reversing this pattern by focusing on the times when you are getting along? What is done differently during these times of compatibility versus the times of disagreement? Answering these questions might provide the clue you need for fewer hassles in the future.

Often when I talk with couples about their conflicts, their attention is on what creates conflict. But I like to know how the conflict ends. Who started it may not be as important as how and why it ends. This concept is called a truce trigger. It is when you shift your attention to the conflict's ending events, rather than its beginning events. The shift may help you discover why and how the conflict started.

Several other steps can break the cycle of conflict in a marriage. First, identify where most of your conflicts occur. Is it in one location? At the dinner table? In the car? In the bedroom? Discover where conflict occurs and change the location. Make it a policy to begin your discussions in a different place. One couple agreed that whenever they were moving into conflict, they would go into the bathroom to deal with the issue at hand. Usually they began to laugh, which helped them begin to resolve the issue.

The next step is discovering when the conflict occurs. Once that's been established, make an arrangement not to discuss issues at that time. Many couples have found it helpful to schedule a time to discuss issues they know have conflict potential. Some couples even create a structure with rules such as setting a timer (you can't talk more than 30 seconds at a time), paraphrasing (to your satisfaction) out loud what you just heard your spouse say before you can talk and holding hands during the discussion.

Here are two more examples of couples who have used various tactics to resolve conflict. One couple purchased two Groucho Marx-style plastic glasses. They would wear the glasses whenever dealing with conflict, which consistently broke their pattern of conflict. Another couple developed a habit of predicting each evening whether the next day would be a good or bad day. At the end of the day, each spouse told the other whether it had been a good or bad day. Because they made this prediction, having a good day was more of a possibility.

# TAKE-AWAY QUESTIONS

1. Describe how your conflicts end.

2. Where do your conflicts usually occur?

3. When do your conflicts occur?

4. Predict whether tomorrow will be a good or bad day. How will it be a good day?


5. Out of the six truths of relationship happiness, which one, if implemented, would immediately impact your marriage?

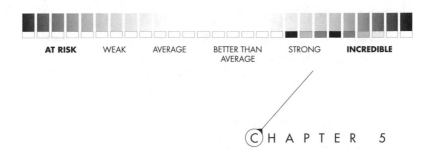

AT RISK    WEAK    AVERAGE    BETTER THAN    STRONG    INCREDIBLE
                               AVERAGE

CHAPTER 5

# When Thoughts Get in the Way

Let's start by reflecting on the Take-Away Questions from chapter 4. Did you discover any patterns of conflict within your marriage? Maybe you were surprised by the fact that you and your spouse always fight at a particular time of day? Or that arguments regularly occur at a certain location? Remember that conflict is part of who we are since the fall of man. It's okay to admit and discover conflict patterns in order to begin taking corrective action. Additionally, when you are answering and discussing questions from this book with your spouse (a great start to correcting negative behavior), consider the following:

You are unique. When asked a question, you will respond through your very own lens. One made up of your past experiences, your beliefs, your personality traits, etc. Your spouse is also unique and has a lens of his or her very own. Therefore, at times, you both may have completely different responses and opinions regarding a conflict or question. And this is okay.

You might be thinking to yourself, *I guess I know that it's okay to disagree with my spouse on different things, but it's very frustrating. At times it leads to conflict that I so desperately try to avoid. What's so good about that?*

Well, it is not that conflict or disagreement is "good" per se but that it just happens. We are a fallen people who sin; therefore, sin is part of who we are. And that is what's so frustrating. This chapter will explain how our sinful nature gets in the way of our marriage relationships and how we can begin to recognize our destructive thoughts and behavior.

## SIN IN OUR LIVES

People often ask me, "What's the cause of most marital problems? Why can't people get along and love one another? What's the main issue?"

I have a simple answer: "The garden."

Usually that response elicits a strange look, so I elaborate with five more words: "The fall of man—sin."

The world still reaps the results of or damage from original sin—in the way we behave, feel and think. And our thoughts are where sin takes root. God pointed this out early in Genesis: "Then the LORD saw that the wickedness of man was great on the earth, and that every intent of the thoughts of his heart was

only evil continually" (Gen. 6:5, *NASB*). In other versions of the
Bible, "thoughts" is translated "imagination." Again, in our minds
is where sin begins.

## Thoughts

I have never been in a hurricane, and I never want to be. The
tremendous force of the violent, swirling winds devastates everything in its path, leaving behind a trail of destruction. But within a hurricane is the eye of the storm—a place of such calm that

> **The eye of the storm exists in
> every person, which can make or
> break a marriage.**

you wouldn't even know about the fury raging around the eye's
perimeter. While it is calm, it still directly relates to the intense,
violent winds that stem outward from the core. Sadly, hurri-
canes pass through many marriages. The eye of the storm exists
in every person, which can make or break a marriage. That eye is
called our thought life, and it is marred. It has an inkling toward
negative thinking as a carryover from the fall of mankind.

Consider these examples:

1. A husband comes home from work early and greets
   his wife with a hug and kiss. But in return she becomes angry and glares at him. Why?
2. A wife returns her husband's overdue books to the
   library, and he becomes annoyed at her for doing so.
   Why?

3. A husband brags about his wife's cooking to a number of friends, and she becomes furious at him for doing so. Why?

In each case, the spouse's positive action induces unexpected reaction from his or her spouse. The anticipated reaction would have been appreciation, not anger. What happened? Why the negative reactions? Let's go back and look at the thoughts each spouse had in response to the positive overture.

In the case of the wife whose husband came home early, she thought, *Why did he come home at this time? Is he checking up on me? If there is anything undone, he'll criticize me. I don't need that.*

The husband with the overdue library books thought, *I was going to take those back. I'm capable of doing that. She's trying to point out that I'm not responsible. She doesn't trust me to follow through, so she's going to jump in and do it herself!*

The wife who was praised for her cooking thought, *He never praises me that much at home. He's just using me to get attention for himself from his friends. He probably wants me to compliment him on something now. I wonder what they think about me now?*

In each case, the reactive negative thoughts just popped into their minds. Has something like this ever happened to you? Probably. But why? Perhaps your thought was based on a past experience, or you were having a difficult day. But in each case, regardless of the intent and purpose of the spouse who did something positive, the reaction was such that it might limit a positive overture another time.

### Labels

Negative thoughts never provide an accurate picture of your spouse. They are limited, biased and slanted in one direction. Paul Coleman writes about labels in his book *The Forgiving*

*Marriage*, and I will highlight some of his key points.

Labeling your spouse with negative titles such as callous, selfish, controlling, insensitive, manipulative, unbending, crazy, etc. creates a one-sided depiction of your spouse. More important, thoughts and labels interfere with one of the ingredients most essential for a marriage to change, progress and move forward—forgiveness. You have to see your spouse in a new light in order for forgiveness to occur. Can you forgive a person after you've thought or labeled him or her negatively?

Labels are false absolutes. They are developed to describe those who are different and to keep us from thinking. Additionally, labels make it easier to justify ourselves. If we used our minds constructively, we would be able to see both sides of a person. Labels limit our understanding of what occurs in a marriage, for we see the label as the cause of the problem. Why look elsewhere?

Labels also keep us from looking at our part in the problem. We use labels to avoid looking in the mirror, for fear of what it will reflect. When you treat your spouse as if he or she is a certain way and possesses a particular quality, he or she may begin to act that way. Our negative thoughts and labels often become self-fulfilling prophecies. We end up cultivating exactly what we don't want to grow.

Do you and your spouse label each other? Are the labels positive and motivating or negative and debilitating? Are they attached to descriptions such as "always" or "never"? If you do label your spouse, consider correcting the label, and in your heart and mind, give him or her an opportunity to be different.[1]

The following example shows how thoughts can put a damper on an otherwise enjoyable occasion and how to interrupt the downhill slide and move it back to an enjoyable level. June and her husband, Frank, went to a movie. Afterward, Frank suggested they walk down to a restaurant for a piece of pie. Let's look inside their minds as the conversation continued:

June's first thought was, *Oh boy. He knows I've been trying to diet and lose weight. He's just thinking of himself as usual. You'd think he'd remember something as important as that.* June responded with an exasperated, "No, I'd rather just go home." Frank thought, *Now what's wrong with her? We had a great time, and now she's getting all bent out of shape. She sure goes up and down with her emotions.* Frank said a bit irritably, "Fine. Just forget it."

They walked to the car in silence, but this time something new was beginning to take place. They were both learning to recognize how their thoughts had been feeding the way they responded to each other. So during their silence, each one was working on challenging their statements or destructive thoughts.

June began to think, *Well, maybe he just didn't think about it. After all, he's not the one on a diet, I am. And he's probably hungry. I could have a cup of decaf.* She also thought, *I guess I would prefer to go home and get some sleep. I've been overworked this month. I guess I must have snapped at him, and I didn't need to. His request was innocent enough.* At the same time Frank thought, *June has been pushing it at work recently. And it is 10:30. Maybe she's tired and wants to go home.* He also thought, *We've worked out other disagreements. I think we can work this one out.*

June, who had calmed down by this time, said, "I didn't need to snap at you. I guess I was thinking about myself a bit too much. I guess I was looking forward to getting some rest. And I realize, too, that you could be hungry."

Frank responded, "I appreciate your clarifying that. I know you've been working a lot. And I just remembered you're on a diet and that eating pie in front of you might make you drool." And with that comment, they both laughed and were relieved because they were learning to turn things around.

Whenever our spouse does something, we can choose to react with a negative interpretation, assumption, suspicion of intent or guarded and defensive manner. On the other hand, we have the choice to respond at face value to what was said or done, give the benefit of the doubt, see it as a positive step and then show appreciation. Of these two choices, the biblical response follows the latter of the two. "Love . . . is ever ready to believe the best of every person" (1 Cor. 13:7, *AMP*). Remember, the choice is yours as to whether you'll allow negative thoughts to generate anger. Not fostering that anger will let it subside. And one way to keep love alive and moving in a positive direction in your relationship is to have full awareness of your thoughts and beliefs toward your spouse. The idea is to first look at your thoughts for a solution when facing a problem or negative situation.

## NAMES YOU CALL ME

The other day I looked up the word "slander" in the dictionary. Do you know what it means? It is the utterance of a false statement, or statements, that is damaging to a third person's character or reputation.[2] It then dawned on me that many of our thoughts about one another fall into this category. And then to think, God knows all of our negative thoughts. Many spouses commit slander in their minds. I have heard many such comments in my counseling office. Unfortunately, some of the thoughts we have about our spouses fall into the category of character assassination rather than character adoration. And this character-assassination style of thinking generates both conflict and distance in our marriage relationships.

Have you ever met an assassin? Probably not. An assassin has one job and one goal in mind. While very few spouses ever physically assassinate their mates, many assassinate them in their minds. As a result, the spouse's character is torn down; in fact, character assassination is a root cause of marital difficulties. On the other hand, character adoration builds up a marriage. Whenever your spouse pleases you, respond in a positive way, either in your mind or aloud to your spouse.[3]

All too often, the problem with what you say to one another (and usually regret later) is a result of minutes or even hours of talking to yourself about your spouse or the situation. Often these thoughts hop in automatically and camouflage themselves amidst other thoughts. The authors of We Can Work It Out call these "hot thoughts" and best describe the thoughts in this way:

Hot thoughts lead to feelings of hopelessness ("He's never going to change"), anger and resentment ("I don't deserve to be treated like this"), and even depression ("All I want to do is stay in bed, watch TV, and eat"). Hot thoughts also lead directly to destructive patterns of relationship talk. If you feel angry and hopeless, you will say things that communicate these feelings. You are likely to criticize your partner, offer negative problem solutions, mind-read your partner's thoughts and feelings, and fail to utilize listening talk. Because these behaviors tend to elicit replies in kind from your partner, you find yourself in the middle of an argument that confirms your worst thoughts. But it's a vicious cycle. Your thoughts lead to actions that increase the chance of conflict, and the inevitable conflicts provide energy for more hot thoughts. You will rapidly find yourself trapped in one or more of the now-familiar patterns of escalation and pursuit—withdrawal.[4]

As you can see, hot thoughts are thoughts to avoid. In order to avoid these thoughts, reach for character adoration over assassination. Adoring your spouse will build a positive and healthy

> **Whatever happens within a marriage relationship reflects the inner workings, whether positive or negative, of each person's mind and heart.**

thought life, which in turn will produce a growing, fulfilling marriage relationship. Let me put it this way: whatever happens within a marriage relationship reflects the inner workings, whether positive or negative, of each person's mind and heart. Remember, positive or negative relationships are your choice.

## ROADBLOCKS THAT STUNT OUR RELATIONSHIPS

Be aware that numerous poor thought patterns exist, and these can deaden and block a marriage relationship. Let's go back to the counseling office so that you can hear some common beliefs that impede progress.

## Assumption

The first roadblock is assuming. Usually, assumptions are nega-tive, portraying the worst in another person. For example, you make unfavorable judgments about your spouse when you hear him or her singing in another room and think, *He's just doing that to irritate me. He knows that bothers me.* However, you don't really know that, because you can't read minds, let alone determine another person's motive.

## Overgeneralization

Another pattern of thinking that is bothersome and difficult to change is overgeneralizing. Statements such as "He never listens to me," "She's always late" or "You never consider what I want" are all forms of overgeneralizing. These types of statements, if directed to your spouse, are most likely plausible if you're upset over a few incidents. In our eyes, our spouses are "always" or "never." So we have condemned them no matter the circum-stance and probably won't give them credit, even when they have done what is important to us. Compare these overgeneralized words to an insecticide that drifts across a field and kills all the crops, rather than just the pests. The insecticide represents the overgeneralizing statement, which poisons and eventually kills our spouse's desire to try to listen or not be late. Unfortunately, the spouse hearing these statements usually gives up.

## Magnification

The third poor pattern of thinking, magnifying, occurs when a person tends to enlarge the qualities of another person, usually in a negative way. Most of the time we think this way when a situa-tion seems out of control. I recall one husband who wasn't at his best when it came to spending and saving money. Once, when some checks bounced, his wife shared some of her thoughts with me: "He is such a spendthrift"; "He does this constantly"; "We won't have enough money for the bills this month"; "If we're late on the house payment again, they'll foreclose"; and finally, "We're going to lose our house, and it's all because of him." I think you can imagine the ensuing conversation.

I've also heard husbands and wives use defeatist beliefs when magnifying—"Nothing can change or improve our relationship." This attitude will not only keep you from taking positive steps forward but also cause you to view your spouse and the relationship through a negative filter. Similar to labeling, magnifying usually evolves into a self-fulfilling prophecy. It is a vicious cycle. Do you know what the results of this pattern are? Let me give you several examples. And even if they don't fit you and your situation, they may affect someone you know.

The defeatist belief spurs on a sense of resignation—"I'll just have to learn to live with this." When you begin feeling powerless, the downward spiral has probably started. You may start thinking less of yourself, which usually leads to thinking less of your spouse. And when this happens, your love and generous spirit toward your spouse begins to dry up.

I remember hearing one husband say, "I'm afraid my learning to live with it was the first step in learning to live without her." This is a sad position to be in, because the majority of situations are capable of being changed and achieving positive growth.

I've also talked with spouses who end up feeling like martyrs. Martyrs usually let their spouse know what negative things they've had to live with. This attitude only brings the spouse down and, in time, the negativity can draw out feelings of revenge. Even if the revenge is hidden or blatant, it still causes the negatives to be set in cement.

# HOPE FOR OUR THOUGHT LIVES

If you or anyone else believe nothing can improve your marriage, test the belief or pattern of thinking you're struggling with. Challenge it. Look at, define and clarify the problems. Then select one problem that appears the easiest to change. For example, one husband just wanted to have discussions with his wife without the usual defensive arguments that seemed to constantly erupt. He and I enjoyed brainstorming different ways he could stay out of the argument in order to eliminate his defensiveness.

- He chose to believe that his wife wasn't out to get him or simply argue with him out of spite. She might actually have some good ideas.
- He committed himself not to interrupt, argue, debate or walk out on her.
- He would respond to what she said by making statements such as "Really," "That's interesting," "I hadn't considered that," "Tell me more" and "I'd like to think about that."
- He also chose to think the following: Even if this doesn't work the first time, I'll try it at least five times.
- He determined to thank her for each discussion, and when her response was even 5 percent less defensive, he would compliment her for her response.

Five weeks later, he called and said, "The fourth discussion was totally different. It's starting to work, Norm. You destroyed my belief that nothing can improve our relationship. There's a bit of hope now." As people have worked at challenging these beliefs and turning negativity into positive energy, I've not only witnessed their personal growth but also the growth in their spouses.

The key to a lot of our problems is the development of hope. Focusing more on God's Word, especially on passages filled with a hope for the future, might help counter our negative and hopeless beliefs. For example, in Jeremiah we read, "'For I know the plans that I have for you,' declares the LORD, 'plans for welfare and not for calamity to give you a future and a hope'" (Jer. 29:11, *NASB*).

We have the choice to change our thought life. And the best way to help us change our thoughts is by applying Scripture to our daily lives.

Scripture tells us to bring into captivity every thought to the obedience of Christ (see 2 Cor. 10:5, *KJV*). All of us at sometime or another need some housecleaning in our minds. Another way of putting this is our minds need renewal. It is important that through renewal, you see or look differently at your spouse. Stephen Covey tells of an experience he had one Sunday morning while riding a subway in New York:

People were sitting quietly—some reading newspapers, some lost in thought, some resting with their eyes closed. It was a calm, peaceful scene. Then suddenly, a man and his children entered the subway car. The children were so loud and rambunctious that instantly the whole climate changed.

The man sat down next to me and closed his eyes, apparently oblivious to the situation. The children were yelling back and forth, throwing things, even grabbing people's papers. It was very disturbing. And yet, the man sitting next to me did nothing.

It was difficult not to feel irritated. I could not believe that he could be so insensitive as to let his children run wild like that and do nothing about it, taking no responsibility at all. It was easy to see that everyone else on the subway felt irritated, too. So finally, with what I felt was unusual patience and restraint, I turned to him and said, "Sir, your children are really disturbing a lot of people. I wonder if you couldn't control them a little more?"

The man lifted his gaze as if to come to a consciousness of the situation for the first time and said softly, "Oh, you're right. I guess I should do something about it. We just came from the hospital where their mother died about an hour ago. I don't know what to think, and I guess they don't know how to handle it either."

Suddenly, I *saw* things differently, and because I *saw* differently, I *thought* differently, I *felt* differently, I *behaved* differently. My irritation vanished. I didn't have to worry about controlling my attitude or my behavior; my heart was filled with the man's pain. Feelings of sympathy and compassion flowed freely . . . Everything changed in an instant."[5]

Like Covey, if you approach a situation with empathetic, rather than negative thinking, feel what another is going through and maintain admiration for the person's good qualities, you won't be plagued with overwhelming distress-maintaining thoughts that trigger defensiveness and harm in your marriage.

## POSITIVE THOUGHTS IN CONTROL

Brace up your mind—that's an interesting thought. It literally means to prepare your mind for action. As believers, we are called to fill our minds with positive thoughts and rid our minds of hindering thoughts, which include those focusing on our failures or the failures of others. Bracing up our minds involves refocusing our thoughts in the direction of what God can do.

In his book *Bringing Out the Best in People*, Alan Loy McGinnis described his Sunday visit to the church in New York that Dr. Norman Vincent Peale pastored for over 50 years. As the aged minister stepped into the pulpit and began to speak, McGinnis realized why the congregation refused to let Dr. Peale retire, even at age 86. He preached a dynamic sermon on the subject of worry and doubt. He told story after story about people, who with the Lord's help, overcame their difficulties.

After the service, McGinnis complimented the pastor on his uplifting message and encouraging illustrations. Dr. Peale said that a number of people had criticized him over the years for telling so many positive stories. However, he continued to use such illustrations, he said, because the Bible says nothing to us about rehearsing failure.[6]

What an interesting concept—rehearsing failure! Many of us live on that stage, constantly mulling over failed memories on the part of our spouse. Instead, we should think about the instances where God worked in their life and how He will continue to work in the future. If you are going to rehearse anything, rehearse what God can do in your and your spouse's lives. And as you look at your spouse, don't think about how he or she has let you down. Such thoughts hold your spouse a captive of the past in your mind. Rather, rehearse good memories and positive expectations—this is what sets spouses free.

If you find this rehearsal of positive memories difficult, start with small steps. Make a list of your spouse's positive qualities— the things he or she does to build up your life together. Memorize this list and think about how much harder life would be without your spouse and his or her positive qualities. When you find yourself following a critical train of thought about your mate, use elements from the list to interrupt your thinking. If you make a habit of this process, the change can be dramatic. You may also want to work on restructuring your habitual thoughts together with your spouse. Going through the process as a team often leads your spouse to more positive thinking too. And once you begin rethinking your marriage, don't keep your positive thoughts to yourself.[7]

You have probably heard about Tony Campolo through his speaking and writing ministry. Consider some thoughts on marriage from the pen of his wife, Margaret:

Remember how much you enjoyed looking terrible in the funny mirrors at amusement parks when you were a child? It was fun because you knew you really did not look like that. You could always find a real mirror and be sure you were you.

In marriage, each partner becomes the mirror for the other. . . . Often a problem in a bad marriage is that one or both of the mirrors is working like those old amusement park mirrors. A spouse begins to reflect ugly things, and the other one feels that his or her best self isn't there any more.

Mirrors reflect in simple ways; people are far more complicated. We choose what we reflect, and what we choose has much to do with what the other person becomes. One of the most exciting things about being married is helping your partner become his or her best self by reflecting with love.

Positive reflecting will make your spouse feel good about himself or herself and about you, but it will also change the way you feel. As you look for the positive and overlook the negative, you will become happier about your marriage and the person you married. This will happen even if your spouse does not change at all!

In a difficult marriage, as in the difficult times of a good marriage, ask God for understanding and the ability to do what is humanly impossible. Jesus is our model. And in reflecting our marriage partners positively we are following His example.[8]

# TAKE-AWAY QUESTIONS

Take a few minutes and write down your thoughts surrounding your marriage and spouse in order to raise your awareness of whether your thoughts promote or hinder growth in your marriage.

1. My positive thoughts about my spouse are:

2. My negative thoughts about my spouse are:

3. Beliefs I have that help my marriage grow are:

4. Beliefs I have that keep my marriage from growth are:

5. Read the following passage from Philippians:

> Finally, brothers, whatever is true, whatever is noble, whatever is right, whatever is pure, whatever is lovely, whatever is admirable—if anything is excellent or praiseworthy—think about such things (Phil. 4:8).

Two examples of each adjective in this passage that apply to my spouse are:

Reflect on your responses and then begin to focus on your positive thoughts until a pattern forms. Follow this pattern daily and note the changes that occur in your marriage.

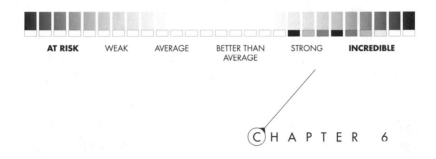

C H A P T E R    6

# Marriage Hang-Ups

Who do you listen to for marital advice? Who or what affects your thought life? Friends? Family? Talk shows? Those who have been married several times? Many couples and individuals listen and find help from nonexperts. However, consider this: Would you listen to a man who has helped more than 2,000 couples over a time span of two decades? Would you listen to a man who because of his research can predict which marriages will succeed and which will fail with a 94 percent accuracy? I would. I'd sit up and listen well.

Dr. John Gottman, professor of psychology at the University of Washington, has conducted numerous studies that reveal that marital happiness does not reside in a particular style of relating to or handling conflict. Gottman concludes that couples leaning toward divorce interact more negatively than positively. While some believe you have to have a certain style of relating to or handling conflict in order to be fulfilled, Gottman shows that it is the balance between positive and negative feelings and behaviors toward one another that really makes the difference. Gottman strongly feels that a marriage is likely to be stable and fulfilling as long as there is five times as much positive feeling and interaction as there is negative.[1]

Gottman's studies ring true. It often seems that positive interactions can mean nothing or are easily forgotten after just one negative, critical remark or behavior. What do you think the positive-over-negative ratio is in your marriage at this time? Please check one of the following positive-over-negative ratios:

❏ 1 to 1    ❏ 2 to 1    ❏ 3 to 1    ❏ 4 to 1    ❏ 5 to 1    ❏ 6 to 0

A marriage needs a higher positive ratio in order to nourish love. Here are some examples of positive interaction:

- Showing interest in one another's lives
- Being affectionate and tender
- Showing you care by thoughtful acts
- Expressing your concern and listening
- Being accepting of a different opinion but respectfully disagreeing when needed (remember the word "respectfully"!)
- Being empathetic through verbal and nonverbal expressions
- Expressing laughter and joy and sharing these together

These are factors that make a marriage work.

How much do positive interactions affect your life together on a scale of 0-10? (Zero indicates very few positive interactions, and 10 indicates consistently positive interactions.)

| 0 | 1 | 2 | 3 | 4 | 5 | 6 | 7 | 8 | 9 | 10 |
|---|---|---|---|---|---|---|---|---|---|----|

What can you do to increase the positive rating on your scale?

Changing our negative patterns of behavior is hard work. It takes time, energy and patience. But most of all, it takes a heart for God and obedience to the Scriptures.

# THE FOUR DESTRUCTIVE FORCES

Dr. John Gottman's studies also revealed the four destructive forces in a marriage—criticism, contempt, defensiveness and stonewalling. He calls them the four horsemen.[2] In Scripture, we know these four horsemen as symbols of destruction (see Rev. 6). The white horse was sent out to conquer. The red horse was sent to wipe peace from the earth. The pale horse represented death and the black horse represented famine.

As these forces invade a marriage, a couple's attention is diverted from the positive to the negative. Each attitude or behavior gains a foothold in the relationship and opens the door for the next horseman to step through and expand the destruction. Actually, these four destructive forces are contaminants. They infect the relationship with a toxic substance that gradually erodes the feelings of love until the marriage is overcome by negativity. When we see these forces described in a couple's relationship, it is possible to predict with a safe amount of accuracy which marriages will most likely end in divorce. That is a bit frightening, isn't it? The good news is that if a couple stops and identifies the destructive forces, they can be removed from their marriage.

## Criticism

Criticism is the first destructive force and probably the most dangerous. Its negative response opens the door for the other destructive forces to follow. Remember, the closer you are to a person who criticizes, such as a spouse, the more it hurts. Spouses are often critical of one another in marriage. Sometimes our criticism of each other is valid, but it is not valid if it springs from a wrong appraisal of our spouse's behavior. While you may not have control over the fact that unjust criticism will come your way, you do have control over how you handle it.

Basically, criticism attacks, blames or fault-finds another person's personality and character. Most criticisms stem from our thought lives. For example, you can attack your spouse by making an overgeneralized statement such as, "You always do this or that." These statements personally accuse, as the word "you" is central to the criticism. On the other hand, criticism takes the form of blame when the word "should" is included in a statement such as, "You should have done it this or that way."

Criticism also hides under the camouflage of joking and humor. When confronted about it, a person usually avoids responsibility by saying, "Hey, I was just joking." It reminds me of the passage in Proverbs that says, "Like a madman shooting deadly, burning arrows is the one who tricks a neighbor and then says, 'I was just joking'" (Prov. 26:18-19, NCV).

Another form of criticism is called invalidation and also causes marital distress. When invalidation exists in a marriage, it destroys the effect of validation or the friendship in the marriage. Sometimes couples get along and maintain their relationships without sufficient validation. However, most couples cannot handle continual invalidation. Invalidation is another example of how one negative comment can destroy 20 acts of kindness, as discussed in chapter 4.[3]

Invalidation is like a slow fatal disease that, once established in a relationship, spreads and destroys the positive feelings. As one wife said, "The so-called friend I married became my enemy with his unexpected attacks. I felt demeaned, putdown, and my self-esteem slowly crumbled. I guess that's why our fights escalated so much. I had to fight to survive."

Criticism is usually destructive in that it accuses, intimidates and tries to make the other person feel guilty. It is often an outgrowth of personal resentment. However, many users of criticism say their remarks are only trying to change their spouses into better people by offering "constructive" criticism. This is a dangerous belief, because all too often criticism does not construct; it demolishes. It does not nourish a relationship; it poisons. And often how the criticism is packaged mirrors this description: "There is one who speaks rashly like the thrusts of a sword" (Prov. 12:18, *NASB*). To keep love in your marriage alive, keep the criticism out of it.

## Contempt

The next step down the path of destruction is contempt—the intent to insult or psychologically abuse your spouse. That sounds harsh, doesn't it? But contempt is what happens when criticism creeps into our marriages. It is like using a mortar in battle to lob shells into the enemy lines, but in marriage, you're lobbing insults, not at enemies, but at the person you promised to love. Negative thoughts cause negative statements to abound. Nothing is sacred. Name-calling, negative nonverbal actions and mocking are all part of the pattern. After contempt enters a marriage, it is difficult to remember your spouse's positive qualities or acts. Think of contempt as character assassination over adoration (discussed in chapter 5). Don't tear down your spouse's character by using contempt; rather, build it up by using love.

## Defensiveness

Contempt brings to the forefront the third force of destruction in a marriage—defensiveness. This is a natural, protective response intended to diffuse attacks coming from the outside. Defensive statements are viewed as excuses and are frequently accompanied by a counterattack. One of the more harmful effects of defensive behavior is its correlation with emotional intimacy. The greater the degree of defensiveness between a couple, the less the amount of emotional intimacy exists in the relationship. Even though your spouse's attack may be grossly exaggerated, unreasonable and unfair, responding defensively will only encourage the walls you've built for protection to stay standing tall. In reality, the walls are what keep you and your spouse emotionally distanced.

## Stonewalling

Stonewalling is the last and worst stage of the four destructive marital forces. At this stage, both spouses will most likely feel they are talking to the brick wall their spouse has built in order to defend themselves. Stonewalling usually elicits little or no response. The loudest sound is silence, and the message it imparts is distance and disapproval. It is a method used more by husbands than by wives. The silent retreat irritates a wife and sends her the message that he doesn't love her. Men tend to avoid conflict in marriage more than wives, and it upsets them more psychologically. When stonewalling turns chronic, it usually sounds the death cry for a marriage, even when just one spouse employs the tactic.

# THE DANGER IN ANGER

We hear about criticism, contempt, defensiveness and stonewalling destroying marriages, but we probably hear more about anger destroying marriages. And anger *out of control* does destroy marriages. Sometimes it is hard to remember that anger in and of itself is not the problem. Anger is an expression of frustration, fear and hurt, and these feelings turn into anger in order to disguise what we are really feeling. Anger is a form of dishonest emotional expression. Remember, anger does not draw a person toward you; rather, it pushes the person away, which creates distance, not closeness. From my observation, anger seems to have even more negative effects in marriage if it is expressed with any of the four destructive forces. It is much healthier for the couple in a relationship to openly and honestly say, "I'm frustrated-angry" or "I'm afraid-angry." You are more likely to receive a listening ear from your spouse than a defensive counter-attack.

If these negatives have become a part of your marriage routine, are you ready to do (not try, but do) something new? After all, if what you're doing now isn't working, why keep on doing it? There is a better way.

Even in strong relationships, people too often focus on the negatives in an attempt to make the relationship all the better. However, by dwelling on what is wrong in your marriage, it is easy to lose sight of what is right. This is a primary reason why admiration is often the first thing to go. Once you allow your spouse's negative qualities to consume your thoughts, you may forget all the attributes you long admired and valued.

To improve or save your marriage, you must remind yourself that your mate's negative qualities do not cancel out all the positive qualities that led you to fall in love. Nor do bad times wipe out all the good times. If your marriage is going through a rocky period, it is particularly important to recall specific happy memories you have of your mate. If this proves difficult, force yourself to sit and think about the positive memories. For example, you could look through picture albums from past vacations

## The bottom line is that you are the architect of your thoughts.

or reread old love letters. Don't forget the advice provided in chapter 5—our thought lives can either promote or hinder growth in our marriages.

The bottom line is that you are the architect of your thoughts. You need to decide what your inner script contains. You have two options: Either look at what your relationship lacks and at your disappointments by filling your mind with thoughts of irritation, hurt and contempt; or do just the opposite. What will you decide?

## STEPS TO OVERCOME THE FOUR DESTRUCTIVE FORCES

We can learn how to positively respond to criticism from studying people in the Bible who were criticized. Looking at the thought lives of biblical men and women will help us overcome the four destructive forces in our marriages.

Looking at Moses, we know he was criticized, not only by the nation God called him to serve, but also by his subordinates. However, the real pain came when his own family criticized him. When Moses married a Cushite woman, his own brother and sister spoke against him (see Num. 12:1). Aaron and Miriam became jealous of Moses and questioned whether God had really spoken through him (see Num. 12:2). They even publicly declared their accusations. This is when criticism really hurts—when family members criticize. Therefore, it is best when a problem occurs between you and your spouse not to bring other family members into it. What usually happens if you get family involved is you get over the problem, but your family hangs on to it for years.

Take a clue from Moses about handling criticism. First, he did not retaliate against his brother and sister. Retaliation is usually the first response to criticism. When you retaliate, you don't solve the problem; you only compound it by becoming like the ones who have hurt you. Second, he did not defend himself against the criticism of his family. He knew that the truth would eventually exonerate him, and it did.

Let's consider what steps you might be able to take when responding to the four destructive forces in marriage. We will focus on criticism, since it is the force that if allowed into a marriage, signals the three other culprits to creep in.

### 1. Realize That Not All Criticism Is Bad

Consider what God's Word has to say about criticism: "It is a badge of honor to accept valid criticism" (Prov. 25:12, TLB). "What a shame—yes, how stupid!—to decide before knowing the facts!" (Prov. 18:13, TLB). "Don't refuse to accept criticism; get all the help you can" (Prov. 23:12, TLB). "A man who refuses to admit his mistakes can never be successful. But if he confesses and forsakes them, he gets another chance" (Prov. 28:13, *TLB*). Don't automatically assume that all negative criticism is invalid.

## 2. Evaluate the Criticism for Validity

I realize that this step may be easier said than done. Looking for value in destructive criticism is sometimes like searching for a needle in a haystack. But you must ask yourself, *What can I learn from this experience? Is there a grain of truth in what I am hearing to which I need to respond?* Asking questions like these will shift you from a defensive position in a relationship to that of an investigator. However unfair your spouse's attack, disregard the negative statements, but don't disregard the heart of the matter. If you give your spouse permission to exaggerate, eventually the exaggerated statements will blow away like chaff, and only the truth will remain. By doing this, you focus on searching for the grain of truth, which will lead you in identifying the real cause for your spouse's critical attack.

## 3. Clarify the Root Problem

Determining precisely what your spouse thinks you have done, or not done, that is bothering him or her, takes great energy on your part because you must look beyond the negative remarks. It is important to understand the criticism from the other person's point of view. Ask specific questions such as, "Will you please elaborate on the main point?" or "Can you give me a specific example?" Suppose your wife says, "You're the most inconsiderate person in the world!" Since this is a very general statement, challenge her to identify specific ways you have acted inconsiderately. Ask for examples from your relationship. Keep digging until the root is exposed. And when this is done, thank her for her observation. As hard as it may be, don't defend or disagree. Thank your spouse, even if you don't feel like it.

## 4. Think About the Charge

At times, the process of investigating accusations and criticisms may overwhelm you with anger, confusion or frustration. Amidst these emotions, your mind may pull a disappearing act— it may go blank! If this occurs, take the time to think before you respond. How do you do this?

First, I need to warn you how not to do it. Don't ask, "Can I take a minute to think about this?" You don't need anyone's permission to take time to think. Also don't say, "Are you sure you are seeing this situation accurately?" This question gives your spouse the opportunity to make another value judgment on the issue. You are vesting him or her with unneeded power.

A better response is, "I'm going to take a few minutes to think this over" or "That's an interesting perspective. I need to think about it." Then ask yourself, *What is the main point my spouse is trying to make? What does my spouse want to happen as a result of our discussion?* Sometimes it is helpful to clarify that point with your spouse by asking, "How would you like me to be different as a result of our discussion? I'm really interested in knowing." And when your spouse tells you (even if their tone isn't what you want to hear), thank him or her.

## 5. Respond Positively and Confidently

Once the central issue or root has been exposed, confidently explain your actions, rather than withering defensively under the attack. I think people who criticize others expect their victims to act defensively, even though these critics sometimes say, "I wish they wouldn't be so defensive when I make a suggestion." In other words, the criticizer is looking for or expecting a fight from the victim. Ironically, when the victim does not act defensively and stand up to the criticism, the critical person is denied a fight, which squelches any further argument or quarrel.

## 6. Agree with Criticism

No matter how hostile or destructive the criticism appears, agree with it to a certain extent. By doing so, you will communicate to your spouse that he or she has been heard and that you are not defensive.

For years with some of the couples I counsel, I have used Manuel Smith's book titled *When I Say "NO," I Feel Guilty*. One of the chapters I incorporate into sessions is based on a technique designed to handle another person's criticism without becoming defensive. This technique is called fogging.[4]

If a husband criticizes his wife as not being adventuresome or not wanting to go out much, she could respond with, "You know, you're probably right. I'm not that adventuresome." When a response like this is given without defensiveness or a counterattack, the potential argument has nowhere to go! There is nothing to fight against because there is no resistance.

Manuel Smith describes this response as similar to a fog bank. Fog in California can be so thick at times that you can't see anything 10 feet away. While the fog appears heavy and sloppy, if you were to throw a rock at the fog bank, it wouldn't stop, bounce off you or bounce back at you but would keep traveling through the fog. The rock has no resistance, even though it appears as if it would encounter a stopping force.

How we accept criticism is like this fog bank. When a spouse criticizes you, his or her criticism will travel right through you if you don't react with either defensiveness or a counterattack.

When you fog, or allow the criticism to pass through unobstructed, you will discover that you listen in a new way. You hear what was said and respond to it at face value. Fogging keeps you from being defensive because you have quit thinking in terms of absolutes. You are now thinking in terms of probabilities *(there is a small probability they are correct)*, instead of thinking in terms of absolutes *(they are correct)*.

# THE CRITICAL REMARK

## Three Invaluable Methods

Coping with criticism is easier said than done. To make it more possible, I would like to introduce three methods that show couples how to deal with criticism and put-downs. The three methods are agreeing with truth, agreeing in principle and agreeing with the odds.

The first one, agreeing with truth, means you listen carefully for any seed of truth in the criticism. Ignore the put-downs or implied derogatory remarks, but agree with the possibility that something is true. Read the following example of a husband sifting through his wife's criticism to get at the truth of the matter regarding his tardiness:

> *Wife*: You're late again. I can never depend on you to be home on time.
> *Husband*: Wow, it's past seven. Time got away from me. You're right. I'm late.

Do you see how the husband decided to ignore the critical remark that he is never home on time, but he acknowledged and admitted his tardiness to his wife? By not acting defensively, the husband prevents further disagreement over the matter.

Agreeing with principle is the second way to deal with criticism. The idea is again to ignore the put-downs or negative remarks but settle on the possibility that what lies at the root of the criticism is a valid principle or point of view. Take a look at the following example of a wife agreeing to a principle that her husband communicates in the form of a criticism:

> *Husband*: It's going to be expensive to hire someone else
> to do all the tree trimming this year if you're not
> going to do it.
> *Wife*: That's true. It will cost more to have someone else
> do this for us.

You can see how the wife prevents further conflict by agreeing with her husband that it would cost more money to hire a tree trimmer. She chooses to ignore his critical comment about the possibility of her not taking on the work.

Finally, agreeing with the odds is similar to the first two methods in that it is necessary to ignore the put-downs or critical remarks. However, the difference with this method is that you assume the odds are in your favor—that what the person said was not meant to offend you but just came across the wrong way.

Implementing these three methods is difficult if your spouse expresses his or her criticisms subtly. When a person's tactic is to sneak critical comments into a conversation, I call those comments sideswipes. One example would be a husband who says, "Most wives I know take the time to fix up their households before their husbands come home at night." When this type of critical remark is made, the wife can respond defensively with, "I fix up when I'm able to do so," "Are you saying I don't?" or "Now what are you criticizing me about?" Or the wife can reply by ignoring the put-down while still listening to the principle. She can say, "Well, that's good that they clean up their households before their husbands get home from work, and it's nice that you notice that." The latter response puts the responsibility back in the husband's lap, forcing him to make a direct request. The latter response will also disarm your attacker, diminishing the possibility of further conflict. You will no longer have a real opponent.

### One More Invaluable Method

Last but not least, the skill and process called penetrating listening reminds me of some of the sophisticated war weaponry in which a bomb or missile penetrates deep within a defensive structure before it explodes. This tactic works because it gets past the initial defense and penetrates to where it will have the greatest effect. Listening that penetrates by going beyond the initial defenses of anger and contempt in a spouse's voice, usually arrives at the core of the concern. Arriving at the core of the concern means you have listened nondefensively, which in turn means you

## Communication is to a marriage what blood is to the body.

will most likely react nondefensively back to your spouse. And when your response is nondefensive, you have not added fuel to the fire, thus squelching any possibility of further argument.

When criticism, contempt, defensiveness and stonewalling become permanent residents in a marriage, they strangle the flow of communication. And communication is to a marriage what blood is to the body. Without it, you die. Begin by taking one of the above-mentioned steps to overcome criticism in your marriage. Who knows, you might just find your defensive walls come tumbling down.

# THE TWO BUILDING BLOCKS

### Appreciation

All couples will voice complaints from time to time. That is normal. So far, we have discussed how criticism and complaints can be voiced in a way that a spouse will hear them and not turn defensive. Now, think of rewording criticisms in a way that tells your spouse how much you'd appreciate a change in him or her. For example, instead of focusing upon what annoys you, talk more about what you would appreciate your spouse doing. Your spouse is much more likely to listen and consider your request if you ride the horse of appreciation, instead of the steed of criticism. Talking critically or negatively only multiplies the probability that your spouse will respond defensively, thus causing an argument. The principle behind pointing toward what you appreciate also conveys to your spouse your belief that he or she is capable of doing what you have requested. Doing this consistently, along with giving praise and appreciation when your spouse complies, will bring about a change.

### Praise

The power of praise cannot be underestimated. I have seen this principle work in raising our golden retriever, Sheffield (not that I'm comparing people to dogs). I trained Sheffield in the basics of obedience by the time he was four months old, and now he brings the paper, takes items back and forth to Joyce and me, "answers" the phone and brings it to me, and picks up items off the floor and puts them in the trash. All it took was ignoring the times when he didn't do it right and giving him praise and hugs when he did do it right.

I don't think people are much different in this respect. Affirming and encouraging responses can literally change a person's life, because we need others to believe in us. An unusual example of this is found in the Babemba tribe of southern Africa. When one of the tribal members has acted irresponsibly, he or she is taken to the center of the village. Everyone in the village stops work and gathers in a large circle around the person. In turn, each person, regardless of age, speaks to the person and recounts the good things he or she has done in his or her lifetime. All the positive incidents in the person's life, plus the good attributes, strengths and kind acts, are praised with accuracy and detail. Not one word about his or her problem behaviors is mentioned.

This ceremony, which sometimes lasts several days, isn't complete until every positive expression has been given by those assembled. The person is literally flooded by positive praises. When the people are finished, the person is welcomed back into the tribe. Can you imagine the person's desire to continue to reflect those positive qualities? Can you imagine how this would make you feel? Perhaps a variation of this is needed in marriages and families today.

Practice what the Babemba tribe does and list at least five strengths or positive attributes of your spouse.

1.
2.
3.
4.
5.

When was the last time you let your spouse know about these? When is the next time you will show your appreciation and praise to your spouse for his or her positive qualities?

## TAKE-AWAY QUESTIONS

Take a moment to read the following passage from Colossians:

Clothe yourselves therefore, as God's own chosen ones (His own picked representatives), [who are] purified and holy and well-beloved [by God Himself, by putting on behavior marked by] tenderhearted pity and mercy, kind feeling, a lowly opinion of yourselves, gentle ways, [and] patience [which is tireless and long-suffering, and has the power to endure whatever comes, with good temper].

Be gentle and forbearing with one another and, if one has a difference (a grievance or complaint) against another, readily pardoning each other; even as the Lord has [freely] forgiven you, so must you also [forgive] (Col. 3:12-13, *AMP*).

Read this passage carefully and use it as an action plan for overcoming criticism in your marriage. As you read it, were you struck by the thought that God is in the clothing business? He tells us what kinds of attitudes, personality traits, etc. to wear. And we can assume that what He tells us not to wear are the exact opposite attitudes, personality traits, etc.

Please answer the following questions to determine if you are wearing the positive qualities of God and His kingdom:

1. In what ways are you expressing tenderhearted pity and mercy? Give two examples.

2. What is one specific expression of this that you will do this coming week for your spouse?

3. In what ways are you expressing kind feelings? Give two examples.

4. What is one specific expression of this that you will do this coming week for your spouse?

5. In what ways are you expressing gentle ways? Give two examples.

6. What is one specific expression of this that you will do this coming week for your spouse?

7. In what ways are you showing patience? Give two examples.

8. What is one specific expression of this that you will do this coming week for your spouse?

9. In what ways are you showing gentleness and forbearance? Give two examples.

10. What is one specific expression of this that you will do this coming week for your spouse?

11. What is it you need to readily pardon in your spouse?

12. What is one specific expression of this that you will do this coming week for your spouse?

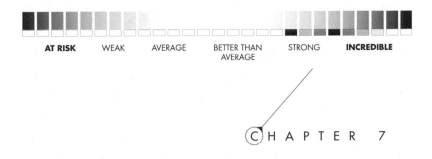

CHAPTER 7

# Forgiveness—The Diet of Champions

We have an abundance of insects in California. One type is rarely seen but definitely makes its presence known. It is the destructive termite. Hidden from view, the termite slowly and steadily feasts its way through the skeletal structure of a house, month after month. The subtle erosion continues and eventually the damage becomes apparent. Then the problem can no longer be ignored. However, by the time the termites' work reaches the visible surface, the internal damage is extensive, and major repairs and expensive reconstruction are often necessary. Some homeowners discover termites as telltale indications of infestation appear. But too many ignore the warning signs and fail to take appropriate steps to evict the invaders.

## DISCOVER THE PEST

In marriage, the four destructive forces of criticism, contempt, defensiveness and stonewalling (as discussed in chapter 6) simulate a breeding ground for its insidious counterpart—the unseen "termite," resentment. This feeling of ill will prevents the growth of oneness, and it simulates a corrosive acid that eats away at the existing relationship. Resentment is usually bred from a real or imagined hurt that we hold against our spouse. The resentful heart operates like a bill-collection agency, making the person pay again and again for what we believe he or she has done. But we often charge so much interest that no matter how earnestly the other person tries to pay the debt, there is always a balance held against him or her. It is a violation of 1 Corinthians 13 (*THE MESSAGE*), which states that love does not keep score.

Resentment costs both of the people in a marriage. It hurts the offender and the offended. But the greatest damage is done to the relationship. Think of resentment like war. In a war, many innocent parents are killed, thus resulting in an abundance of orphans. Similarly, in a marriage, the relationship becomes the orphan as the two spouses engage in their war of resentment. As you can see, allowing resentment into a marriage relationship causes destruction. If you or your spouse are struggling with resentment, it is imperative that you deal with the problem early on. As a termite exterminator often says, "If you had called us sooner, it would have been much easier and less expensive to eliminate the problem." So it is with resentment that is not dealt with early on.

## KNOW THE PEST'S DIET

In your marriage there will always be disappointments, hurts and unmet needs and expectations. After all, you married an imperfect person (and, by the way, so did your spouse). How do you handle your and your spouse's imperfection? Do you look to God and His Word for help, or do you feed on feelings of resentment?

Let's peek into the thought lives of different people who feed the pest of resentment with foods such as revenge, bitterness and anger.

## Revenge

Individuals who struggle with resentment often cannot forgive a spouse's failures. Once a person reaches this point, revenge runs its course. A revengeful spouse makes hurtful comments such as, "You hurt me! You owe me! You must pay! I'll get even with you!" However, what the spouse does not realize is that he or she can never get even. Lewis Smedes tells why getting even is just not possible. "Revenge never evens the score, for alienated people never keep score of wrongs by the same mathematics."[1]

## Bitterness

Have you ever tasted a bitter substance that made you say "Yuck," as well as put a sour, unpleasant look on your face? If your answer is yes, then you've probably tasted the harshness of bitterness. A bitter person will use his or her sharp tongue to cut another person to shreds. In the person's heart and mind, he or she resents the other person so much that he or she is ready to fly off the handle at the slightest provocation. You can just imagine what this does to a marriage. For example, look at Bill. He has been married for three years and has harbored resentful feelings all the while. He exclaims, "I'm so mad! My wife doesn't know what a compliment is! She never notices what I do, and I feel she takes all my work around the house for granted! She should have married a construction engineer."

Do you see how Bill's bitterness toward his wife causes anger and fury, which in turn causes him to become more resentful? It is as if Bill is keeping score with the desire to get back at his wife. He counts plus marks for all his positive behaviors toward his wife, but he then proceeds to count minus marks for all his wife's negative behaviors toward him. Bitterness is a vicious cycle that only feeds our resentments, causing strife between the ones we love.

Have you ever met someone who is antagonistic? If yes, then you have probably met someone like Bill, and you probably cringe at his anger and fury. I would define his statement as an explosive outburst. Anger and fury combined with bitterness is not a good combination. You might as well slap a large chunk of plastic explosives onto a marriage.

## Anger

Do you understand what a quarrel is? It is defined as verbal strife in which the emotions or anger takes over. When anger takes over, you do not focus on resolving the issue at hand but, instead, attack the other person.

But isn't quarreling part of marriage? Absolutely not. Disagreement is okay and bound to happen, but quarreling is forbidden by Scripture. If a person is not a Christian, we wouldn't expect him or her to follow this teaching. However, if you have a personal relationship with Jesus Christ, you are expected not to quarrel. Scripture is quite clear about this:

> It is an honor for a man to cease from strife and keep aloof from it, but every fool will quarrel (Prov. 20:3, *AMP*).
>
> As coals are to hot embers and as wood to fire, so is a quarrelsome man to inflame strife (Prov. 26:21, *AMP*).
>
> Starting a quarrel is like breaching a dam; so drop the matter before a dispute breaks out (Prov. 17:14).

The quarreling or brawling mentioned in the Scriptures depicts images of people who lose control so much so that they inflame strife and breach dams due to quarrels. What I find so shocking is that the Scriptures tell us the awful results of quarreling, but we still carry on the disobedient behavior toward our spouses. While anger might seem more understandable between enemies, it is shocking that we quarrel with the person we love the most. It just does not make sense. The only conclusion we have is that we do what does not make sense because we are of a sinful nature (see chapter 5). Let's begin to look to God and ask Him for continual aid and support to keep us from our fleshly, earthly faults and desires.

## TRY A NEW DIET

All of the examples of resentful people mentioned above were offended, whether it was a legitimate offense or not. Altercations, differences and offenses frequently occur between individuals, families and even nations. Apologies, clarifications of issues, truces and peace treaties make it possible for individuals and nations to live unhindered and unaffected by conflict. But does peace really occur? Does a resolution of differences really take place, or is superficial peace and harmony tainted by lingering inner resentment?

Well, let's take a look. Nations often agree to stop their hostilities and sign peace treaties. However, these peacemaking formalities do not necessarily change warlike attitudes. For example, years after World War I ended, seething resentment eventually fanned the flames of World War II. Another example is when a spouse attempts an apology and even gives a gift to show his or her good intentions, and his or her spouse says, "Oh, that's alright. Let's just forget it happened." But inwardly he or she still feels cold and unforgiving. It is when in the depths of our hearts we do not let go of the cold and unforgiving feeling that the iceberg of resentment freezes intimacy between a couple.

**Taste God's Word**
One passage from Scripture, if permeated into your marriage, could act as the foundational support for a healthy, God-focused marriage. Take a look:

> Let all bitterness and indignation and wrath (passion, rage, bad temper) and resentment (anger, animosity) and quarreling (brawling, clamor, contention) and slander (evil-speaking, abusive or blasphemous language) be banished from you, with all malice (spite, ill will, or baseness of any kind). And become useful and helpful and kind to one another, tenderhearted (compassionate, understanding, loving-hearted), forgiving one another [readily and freely], as God in Christ forgave you (Eph. 4:31-32, *AMP*).

This passage tells you what to do and what to stop doing. That is about as basic as it gets, isn't it? Unfortunately, we are a society used to doing things our own way. We do not appreciate being told what to do and what not to do. However, we all have a sinful nature that needs God's direction. Obviously, God wants to make sure we rid our minds, bodies and spirits of all that would prevent us from becoming loving to one another. Why?

Well, if you take the time to act out these verses in your life, not only your life but also the lives of those around you will change. The benefit of living out these verses is not really seeing the other person change but experiencing the satisfaction from following God's instructions and discovering the difference it makes in your life. God even tells us that when we forgive an offense, love abounds; but if we do not, we separate even close friends (see Prov. 17:9, *AMP*).

### Taste God's Grace

We are called to have a goodness of heart toward others. When you are kind, it comes from a heart of compassion, as discussed in Colossians 3:12. And when you are kind, forgiveness is easier as an act of grace on your part. Just as the Lord forgave me, so must I also forgive (see Col. 3:13). Additionally, it is not just the act of forgiveness we need to perform, but we need to perform the act freely, generously, wholeheartedly, spontaneously and eagerly. We are called to forgive because we have tasted God's grace and forgiveness in our lives.[2]

# COMMIT TO THE DIET

When you decide to go on a diet, you make a decision to stop eating certain foods in order to achieve a desired goal. This same principle of going on a diet applies to many issues in our spiritual lives. For example, if you decide to stop harboring resentful feelings, then you make the decision to let go of those feelings in order to achieve the desired goal of forgiveness. However, the question many people ask when dieting is, "How do I stay committed and faithful to my diet?" How can we stay committed and faithful to ridding our lives of all resentful feelings?

We are on our way to commitment and faithfulness if we first answer this question, Do I let go of my resentments or do I want revenge? Many married individuals struggle with forgiving their spouse or letting them off the hook. With one foot on the road to forgiveness and the other on the road to revenge, a person is immobilized. So the first step involves making a commitment one way or the other. Why divide your energy? Why be halfhearted?

If the part of you that seeks revenge against your spouse is stronger than the forgiving part, then how are you going to get revenge? Does your spouse know of your resentment? Is he or she aware of your craving for some kind of vengeance? Have you written out your plan of attack, with specific details of what you will do? Have you bluntly told your spouse about your feelings and your plans to get back at him or her? If not, why not? If revenge is what you want, why not get it over with and free yourself, so your life can be full and unrestricted? Why not commit wholeheartedly to a life of revenge?

Now you must be thinking, *What? You're crazy! What a ridiculous idea! How could you suggest such a thoroughly unbiblical idea? I would never want to do that, and even if I wanted to, I couldn't do it.* Really? Then why not embrace the other alternative by giving up every ounce of resentment and committing yourself wholeheartedly to a life of forgiveness?

*This is more like it. I want to commit to a life of forgiveness.* Okay, so you want to commit to forgiveness. Remember that giving up resentment is like giving up the sweets you promised you would not eat once you began dieting. It will challenge you. Sometimes giving up resentment means you are giving up having someone else to blame for the predicaments you are in, feeling sorry for yourself and talking negatively about another person. While forgiveness costs a payment or two, the price tag of resentment demands a lifetime of payments.

Finally, think about this: When you hold resentment over someone, you have given him or her control of your emotional state. How do you feel about this? Most of us want to feel like we are in control of our emotions. But you are not in control if you resent someone! You have shifted the power source to someone else. You are letting another person push your emotional buttons of revenge, bitterness and anger. Instead, give your feelings

## Let Jesus be the source of protein in your new and fulfilling diet.

to Jesus Christ and allow Him to work in your life. Let Jesus be the source of protein in your new and fulfilling diet.

## STEP TOWARD FORGIVENESS

The first step in relinquishing resentment is to become aware of and identify the emotions holding you prisoner. The second step is to forgive yourself for harboring resentment toward others. The third and final step is to forgive the significant people of your past for being who they were (and perhaps still are). Please remember that these steps are easier said than done. It will take time, energy and patience to complete all three steps.

What are some of the benefits of relinquishing resentment? Love, intimacy and romance to name a few. For example, look at what love promotes in a marriage: Love frees you to disagree with what your spouse says or does without becoming resentful. You learn to communicate honestly. Additionally, change in your attitude may help your spouse change.

While multiple ways exist to overcome and release resentment, I use an approach in my counseling office that incorporates some of the better techniques currently practiced by various therapists.[3] I hope these suggestions will be effective for you. Keep in mind that if your marriage is hindered from past hurts, these techniques can effectively release resentment whether the person(s) involved is living or deceased.

**Method One**

The first method I use for people to relinquish resentment is a written and verbal exercise. Let's put this exercise into practice. First, list all the resentments you hold toward your spouse. Itemize each hurt or pain you recall in as much detail as possible. Write down exactly what happened and how you felt about it then and how you feel about it now. To aid you in the process, look at some examples from two of my clients.

One client shared the following list of resentments:

- I feel hurt that you made sarcastic remarks about me in front of others.
- I feel hurt that you found it hard to ever give me approval.
- I resent that you wouldn't listen to me.

Another client shared:

- I hate the fact that you called me trash and treated me the same.
- I feel offended by the way you try to use me for your own benefit.
- I resent you for not loving me for who I am. You're always trying to change me into some unreal image.

Please be aware that you may experience some emotional turmoil as you make your list. Many have shared that as they face the resentments they hold toward their spouse, other buried feelings and experiences from their childhood come to mind. If this happens, you may need to repeat this exercise for others in your past.

While completing the exercise, ask God to reveal to you the deep hidden pools of memory so that all your inner resentments can be flushed out. Thank Him for revealing these feelings and allowing you to expel them from your heart and mind. Visualize Jesus Christ in the room with you, smiling and giving His approval to what you are doing. Imagine Him saying to you, "I want you to be cleansed and free. You no longer need to be emotionally crippled because of what happened to you."

After you have thoroughly verbalized your resentments in writing, spend time formulating how you will share the list with your spouse. Practice reading your list aloud. Then select an appropriate time to discuss the list with your spouse. When sharing, be sure to request improvements for your spouse to make in the future. Always point toward the desired positive behaviors.

On the other hand, some individuals find it too difficult to share a list of resentments with their spouse. If you find yourself in this position, employ an intermediate approach of sharing your list when your spouse is not present. Prepare a quiet, comfortable room with two chairs facing each other. Spend a few moments in prayer, asking for the guidance of the Holy Spirit and the presence of Jesus Christ. Imagine Jesus coming into the room, walking up to you, smiling at you and telling you that He loves you and your spouse, and that He wants you to be free from your resentments. He then encourages you to proceed.

Sit down in one of the chairs and imagine that your spouse is sitting in the other. Begin reading your list to the other chair as if your spouse were present. As you read, imagine that your spouse thoughtfully accepts what you verbally share. Imagine your spouse listening to you, nodding in acceptance and under-standing your feelings.

At first you may feel awkward and even embarrassed about reading to an empty chair. But these feelings will pass. In the process of reading your list, you may find yourself expanding on what you have written. You may become very intense, angry, depressed or anxious as you rehearse these details aloud. Be sure to verbalize these feelings with as much detail as possible. Remember, not only is your nonpresent spouse giving you per-mission to share all of your feelings, but Jesus Christ is also encouraging you to get these inner resentments out.

You may also find that talking through just one topic of resentment will be plenty to handle in one sitting. If you find yourself becoming emotionally drained, don't worry. Just stop, rest and relax. Then resume the normal tasks of the day and come back to your list of resentments at another time, when you are fresh and composed.

Finally, before concluding either method of sharing, close your eyes and visualize yourself, your spouse and Jesus standing together with your arms around one another's shoulders. Spend several minutes visualizing this scene. You may wish to imagine the resented person verbally accepting what you have said to him or her. This is important since your spouse may not accept what you say and instead become angry. However, your spouse's reac-tion is not the purpose behind this exercise. What is important is that you are more aware of your resentment, which will help you identify and release your resentment.

As you complete this exercise, you may notice that even though the exercise is directed toward your spouse, you may uncover other existing hurts from parents or past relationships. Again, you may need to follow this written and verbal exercise for other relation-ships in which you harbor resentment. In fact, forgiving your spouse may hinge on first forgiving others. Repeat this exercise as often as necessary to empty your mind of all resentment.

## Method Two

Another helpful method for releasing resentment is to write a letter to the offending person. This letter, however, is never to be delivered. It is a tool for you to express your resentful feelings in a more personal and detailed fashion than a list.

Start your letter with a salutation, as you would any other letter. However, for the rest of the letter, don't concern yourself with style, neatness, proper grammar or punctuation. Instead, use your energy to concentrate on identifying, releasing and expressing your feelings in great detail.

Like many people, you may find it difficult to start; but as you press on, you will sense your feelings and words beginning to flow out. This is good, so don't hold back! Let out all the bad feelings that have been churning inside you. Don't stop to evaluate whether the feelings you express are good or bad, right or wrong. The feelings are present and need to be expressed. If you find the process emotionally draining, complete the letter in stages over several days.

I ask many of my clients in therapy to write such a letter at home and bring it to their next session. Often they hand me the letter as they enter the room. "No," I say. "I'd like you to keep the letter and we will use it later." At the appropriate time I ask him or her to read the letter aloud to an empty chair in the room, imagining that the resented person is there listening.

I recall one client who wrote an extensive letter to her mother. She was surprised when I asked her to read it in my presence. During the first 15 minutes of reading, my client was very broken and tearful. But through the last five minutes, her weeping ceased and a positive, bright lilt to her voice concluded the letter.

Her reading of the letter worked for the good, as some very painful issues from her past were successfully exposed and dealt with.

**Method Three**
This method is different in that it is administered to those who have completed or at least started the process of relinquishing resentment. This method is the final step necessary for completely releasing resentment. Not only is it important to express and give up feelings of resentment, but it is also essential that you project a positive response to the individual who has wronged you. Discarding your inner resentment is only half the battle, because once empty, the place where you once harbored those ill feelings needs to be filled with feelings and expressions of love, acceptance, forgiveness and friendship.

I have had a number of clients state that they have neither positive nor negative feelings toward certain individuals. They are blasé. But what they have really developed is a state of emotional insulation toward those people. And insulation usually means a blockage of some sort. Neutrality must be replaced by positive, productive feelings.

This exercise will help you develop a positive response toward individuals you resent, which is a means of finding any leftover feelings of resentment and eliminating them. First, take a blank sheet of paper and write your spouse's full name at the top. Below the name write a salutation. Under the salutation write, "I forgive you for . . . ," and complete the sentence by writing down everything that has bothered you over the years. For example, someone might write, "I forgive you for always trying to control my life."

Next, stop to capture the immediate thought that comes to mind after writing the statement of forgiveness. Does the thought contradict the concept of forgiveness you just expressed?

Do you feel an inner rebuttal or protest of some kind? Is there any anger, doubt or caustic feeling that runs against your desire to forgive? Write all these contradictory thoughts immediately below your, "I forgive you for . . . " statement. Do not be surprised if your thoughts are so firm or vehement that it appears you have not done any forgiving at all. Continue the exercise by writing, "I forgive you for . . . " statements, followed by your immediate thoughts, even if they are contradictory.

Keep repeating the process until you have drained all the pockets of resistance and resentment. You will know you have reached that point when you can't think of any more contradictions or resentful responses to the statement of forgiveness you have written. Some people finish this exercise with only a few contradictory responses. Others have a great deal of resentment and use several pages to record their feelings.

The following is a typical example of how a husband forgave his wife for her coldness toward him and her extramarital affair. Notice how his protest and contradictions to forgiveness become progressively less intense. Eventually, his resentment drains away to a point where he can finally say, "I forgive you," and feel no further need for rebuttal.

Dear Liz, I forgive you for the way you've treated me over the years and for your unfaithfulness.
*I'm just saying that. I can't forgive you right now. I'm so hurt.*

Dear Liz, I forgive you for . . .
*How do I know I can trust you after what you did?*

Dear Liz, I forgive you for . . .
*How do I know you're going to be any different? I can't take your coldness anymore.*

Dear Liz, I forgive you for . . .
*I'm really hesitant to open myself up to you anymore.*

Dear Liz, I forgive you for . . .
*I do love you, but I've been rejected so much. I'm afraid of being rejected again.*

Dear Liz, I forgive you for . . .
*I would like to forgive you at times. I don't like these feelings I have.*

Dear Liz, I forgive you for . . .
*It's a bit better as I write this. I feel a bit funny and awkward as I do this.*

Dear Liz, I forgive you for . . .
*I wish this had never happened.*

Dear Liz, I forgive you for . . .
*I know I've blamed you and I feel you're responsible. But maybe I contributed to the problems in some way.*

Dear Liz, I forgive you for . . .
*My anger is less and maybe someday it will go away.*

Three days later after writing this letter to Liz, Jim repeated the exercise. In his second letter, after writing eight contradictory thoughts, Jim was able to conclude with several "I forgive you . . . " statements with no rebuttals.

After completing your own version of this exercise, sit opposite an empty chair as described earlier. Visualize the resented person sitting in the empty chair and verbally accepting your forgiveness. Take as long as you need for this step, because it is very important. Why? Because we cling to our past hurts and nurse them, and in so doing, we experience difficulty in the present with our spouse. We are actually trying to pull rank on God

## Our lack of forgiveness fractures our relationships not only with others but with God as well.

when we refuse to forgive our spouse or ourselves—something He has already done. Our lack of forgiveness fractures our relationships not only with others but with God as well. With this in mind, after the exercise and without showing your list to anyone, destroy your list as a symbol that "old things are passed away; behold, all things are become new" (2 Cor. 5:17, *KJV*).

## ENJOY FORGIVENESS

Sometimes I wonder whether we really know what forgiveness is. Forgiveness costs. It hurts. It doesn't always come easily. Forgiveness cannot be sincere if expressed out of fear. Sincere forgiveness is expressed out of love and compassion. Forgiveness is an action that lets the other person know he or she is loved "in spite of." Forgiveness is no longer allowing what has happened to poison you. Sometimes you feel as though forgiveness isn't deserved. But it never is. That is what makes it forgiveness. It unfolds as a decision to accept what you never thought would be acceptable. And negative thoughts and labels (as discussed in chapter 5) block that decision.

Consider Paul Coleman's thoughts on forgiveness from his book *The Forgiving Marriage*:

In forgiveness, you decide to give love to someone who has betrayed your love. You call forth your compassion, your wisdom, and your desire to be accepting of that person for who he or she is. You call forth your humanness and seek reunion in love and growth above all else.

Forgiveness is the changing of seasons. It provides a new context within which to nurture the relationship. The changing of the seasons allows you to let go of all that has been difficult to bear and begin again. When you forgive, you do not forget the season of cold completely, but neither do you shiver in its memory. The chill has subsided and has no more effect on the present than to remind you of how far you've come, how much you've grown, how truly you love and are loved.

When forgiveness becomes a part of your life, little resentment is left. Anger may not vanish immediately, but it will wither in time. The hot core of bitterness that was embedded firmly in your being burns no more.

Forgiveness comes first as a decision to act lovingly, even though you may feel justified to withhold your love.[4]

In essence, forgiveness is a decision to wish another person well, to call upon God to bless him or her, and to show His grace to the person in a special way.

Forgiveness means saying, "It's alright; it is over. I no longer resent you or see you as an enemy. I love you, even if you cannot love me in return." When you refuse to forgive, you inflict inner torment upon yourself, and all it does is make you miserable and ineffective. You feel hopeless. But when you forgive someone for hurting you, you perform spiritual surgery on your soul. You cut away the wrong that was done to you. You see your "enemy" through magic eyes that now heal your soul. Separate the person from the hurt and release the hurt.

Once this is done, invite that person back into your mind, fresh, as if a piece of history between you and this person has been erased, its grip on your memory broken. Reverse the seemingly irreversible flow of pain within you.[5]

Remember, we are only able to forgive because God has forgiven us. He has given us a beautiful model of forgiveness in Christ's redemptive sacrifice. Allowing God's forgiveness to permeate our lives and renew us is the first step toward wholeness. And the eradication of the barrier of resentment allows your marriage to grow.

Forgive one another as quickly and thoroughly as God in Christ forgave you (Eph. 4:32, *THE MESSAGE*).

## TAKE-AWAY QUESTIONS

Can you accept your spouse for who he or she is, whatever that person may have done?

Acceptance means forgiving to the point that you no longer allow what has occurred in the past to influence you. Only through complete acceptance can you be free—free to develop yourself, to experience life, to communicate openly, to love yourself and your spouse entirely.

1. Where are you in terms of handling your resentment?

2.  Do you need to become aware and identify your resentment by following methods one or two?

3.  Or are you aware of your resentment and now need to fill your empty container with expressions of love by using method three?

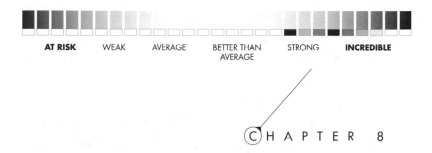

AT RISK     WEAK     AVERAGE     BETTER THAN     STRONG     **INCREDIBLE**
                                           AVERAGE

ⒸH A P T E R    8

# Discovering
# What Works

Since you took the satisfaction- and communication-level surveys to determine where your and your spouse's marriage
currently stands, we have discussed the differences in love languages, the inevitably of conflict in our marriages (due to our
sinful nature), the four destructive marital forces and the idea
that we can terminate resentment through forgiveness.
Throughout these chapters, I hope you have been able to use the
reflective and discussion-based questions in the Take-Away sec-
tions to begin bridging the gap between where you currently
stand in your marriage and where you want to go. The goal of
this chapter is to complete that bridge you've constructed by

providing you with positive methods that can make your marriage successful. The suggestions I am going to give you work. I have seen them work in the lives of couples. The ideas come from many different sources, and I want to pass them along in order to help others. And remember, to focus on the positives, you first need to reach the stage of forgiveness. If you are not there yet, please continue to seek the Lord and ask Him to reveal to you what is holding you back.

Discovering what works in a marriage sometimes only comes after we have found out what does not work. This type of situation reminds me of someone buying a car, boat or computer and then discovering it doesn't work. Frustration, anger and a number of other feelings are sure to erupt. There is nothing quite as frustrating as something not living up to what you thought it was supposed to be. But like a car that is hitting on just seven of its eight cylinders, all that might be needed is an adjustment. However, to make the adjustment, you need to take your car to a mechanic who knows what to do. And you need to follow his advice and suggestions. So it is with a broken piece of a marriage. We need to fix the piece by seeking expert help and advice, whether it be a book, counseling session or a quiet time with the Lord.

## SEE THE GOOD THINGS

If I were to meet you and talk with you about your marriage, I would ask you one question: "What's working?" It is a simple yet significant question.

If I held a marriage seminar with 100 couples and asked everyone the question, "What are the problems and difficulties in your marriage?" how would you picture the responses? I picture a dark cloud of doom and despair.

However, if I were to ask every couple at a session, "What's working for you?" what a different atmosphere and outcome we would have following the meeting. Couples would feel encouraged and challenged by what they heard. They would discover new ways to revitalize their own marriages.

Let me turn to sports for a minute. I enjoy baseball. Sometimes even the best hitters fall into a hitting slump, and they try and try to break out of it. They consult with their hitting coach and analyze what they are doing wrong, so they can get back on track. Many will get videos of themselves while batting to see what they can learn. And it is usually the videos they select that will make the difference. Some will look at videos shot when they were in a slump, and they watch their worst performances. They think that if they focus on what they are doing wrong, they will find and correct the problem. Unfortunately, this does not work well for most hitters.

Other hitters select videos that show a previous hitting streak—when they are doing fantastic. They watch and observe what worked. They soon reach that level again by concentrating on what was working.

Marriage works in a similar fashion. The best step any couple can take is to be like the hitters who focus on what works. This is the best way to solve problems. I am sure there are many times when you and your spouse get along. Can you describe specifically what you and your spouse do differently when you get along? Think about it. Then identify it.

## FOCUS ON THE EXCEPTIONS

I have heard many couples in counseling say, "We don't communicate." Often I ask about the times when they do communicate, which is my way of asking couples to point out the exceptions.

Sometimes I have to be persistent and keep asking, especially when couples are full of pain and despair. At times the progress is slow, but soon I hear an exception to "We don't communicate." (Actually, a couple cannot not communicate. Even silence is an expression of communication.)

One husband finally found an exception and said, "Last Sunday right after church we went out to lunch, just the two of us, and we talked alright. It wasn't bad." After the husband found one exception, the couple was able to come up with several others. And what happened is that these exceptions began to counter the absolute belief that "We can't communicate." For any couple, finding exceptions is the first step in building a sense of hope and optimism. The exceptions begin to diminish the problems.

Focusing on the exceptions also helps couples see their spouse as capable of change—this is especially so for those who have been married longer. As you talk about exceptions, you discover that under certain conditions and circumstances, your spouse is different. As one wife shared, "I used to believe that Jim wasn't interested in sharing his feelings with me. But when we go away on a trip for a few days, and especially when we get away from that darn phone, he seems to relax and get his mind off of work. Those are times when he does open up. I wish that somehow we could create those conditions more frequently." And in time they did, because she discovered that some changes were possible when the setting was right.

Another benefit of focusing on exceptions is that they provide a road map showing how to get to the point where positives increase in a marriage. Following the map and finding the exception might be the window a couple needs to improve their relationship. It may help them develop a plan. So much of what happens in counseling is plan making. This was drilled into me by a man I studied under in the late 1960s—Dr. William Glasser. Since then I have never forgotten the importance of planning. However, the plan must be individualized for your relationship. Jim and Renee are an example of a couple with a plan.

Jim and Renee were a middle-aged couple with a stagnant marriage. Fortunately, they realized this, and one day they each stayed home from work. They went to a small restaurant that was out of the way and quiet. They told the waitress they needed a booth for several hours and would be eating both breakfast and lunch. They also promised a healthy tip. When asked why they did this, Jim said, "We wanted to get out of the house and find a neutral area, and the restaurant was cheaper than a hotel room. Plus, being in public probably kept us from getting overly upset."

During this time, they both talked about how they wanted their marriage to be different a year from now. After they agreed on what they wanted, they identified three to five steps they both would take in order to reach their goal. Then they agreed to take one evening on the 15th of each month to go out to dinner in order to measure their progress and refine their plan. The plan worked, and it was much more economical than seeking assistance from a marriage counselor.

The final benefit of focusing on an exception is that it might enable you to discover a strength; in turn, the strength will build your relationship. Finding strengths is encouraging because it lets a couple know they have been doing something right after all. Perhaps this is an example of what Paul was talking about when he said,

> Whatever is true, whatever is worthy of reverence and is honorable and seemly, whatever is just, whatever is pure, whatever is lovely and lovable, whatever is kind

and winsome and gracious, if there is any virtue and excellence, if there is anything worthy of praise, think on and weigh and take account of these things [fix your minds on them] (Phil. 4:8, *AMP*).

We as Christians are called to be people of hope, rather than despair. We are called to be people who confront obstacles. Finally, we are called to be people who find a way to overcome, rather than resign ourselves to, futile means.

## We as Christians are called to be people of hope, rather than despair.

It is strange, but I have found that some people don't really want to discover the exceptions to the problem. Perhaps they don't want to hope, for fear they will be disappointed. Some see the exceptions as just that—rarities that just happened. Be cautious of selective remembering, because it is then that painful experiences tend to lock in and persist. We do not want to be a people who emphasize failure instead of success, and we do not have to be this way. We can choose another direction. Let's consider the steps that numerous marriage counselors have offered to assist couples in finding fulfilling relationships.

## FOLLOW THE STEPS TO SUCCESS

I have never worked with a couple that does not get along some of the time. We all get along part of the time, even though I realize for some it might be only a little of the time. That is alright. It is enough.

## Identify Your Best Experiences

In order to have a lasting marriage, the first step is discovering what each of you does during the times you get along. Think about this by yourself or with your spouse. Brainstorm and figure out what each spouse was doing before and during that time. Be sure to concentrate more on what you were doing than on what your spouse was doing. This is the beginning point for any change. What were you thinking and feeling when you were getting along? Then plan to do more of it, regardless of what your spouse does. Remember the level of satisfaction chart you plotted in chapter 1. Your chart will help you identify the best experiences in your marriage over time. Here is an example of one husband's chart and evaluation. The asterisk (*) indicates his level of satisfaction.

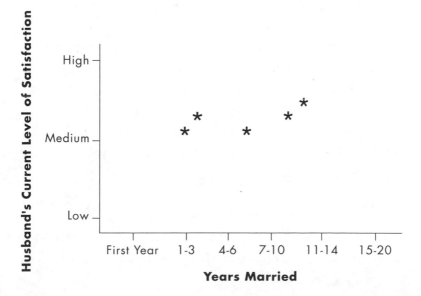

Here is the husband's chart analysis of his best experiences:

- Second year—I felt loved and accepted by you. You had an interest in me and my work.
- Third year—I think you needed me to help with Jimmy, and that was a good experience.
- Sixth year—Seemed to communicate real well without fighting for a few weeks.
- Eighth year—Started praying together twice a week.
- Ninth year—Had a weeklong vacation with no kids or in-laws. We talked a lot and made love every day.

If you haven't plotted and evaluated your best experiences, go back to chapter 1 and do so. It is a great way to discover what worked in the past and to recall and learn from it in order to put it into practice now.

Perhaps all couples need to ask themselves, "During the positive times in our marriage, what did we enjoy doing that we haven't been doing?" Positive behaviors and responses create positive feelings. Biblically we are called upon to behave in specific ways, and nowhere does it ever say to wait until you feel like doing it. Remember the key forgiveness passage in Ephesians 4:31-32. Read as well Colossians 3:12-13, "Therefore, as God's chosen people, holy and dearly loved, clothe yourselves with compassion, kindness, humility, gentleness and patience. Bear with each other and forgive whatever grievances you may have against one another."

## Request Positive Behavior

I refer to the second step for increasing positive behavior between couples in both counseling sessions and seminars as caring behaviors or cherishing behaviors.

First, ask each other, "What would you like me to do for you to show how much I care for you?" The answer must be positive, specific and something that can be performed daily. The purpose behind each request must be to increase positive behavior, not to decrease negative behavior. Look at the following examples:

- "Please greet me with a hug and a kiss" is positive.
- "Don't ignore me so much" is negative.
- "Please line the children's bikes along the back wall of the garage when you come home" is more specific and better than "Please train the children to keep their bikes in the proper place."
- Ted would like Sue "to sit next to him on the sofa when they listen to the news after dinner." This is positive and specific. It is better than asking her to "stop being so preoccupied and distant" (a negative and general request).
- Sue would like Jeff "to kiss her good-bye when they part in the morning." This is positive and specific, which is different from "stop being so distant and cold" (also a negative and general request).

Try making a request or two yourself. Before you make your requests, avoid vague comments by first writing down your answers to the question, "What would you like me to do for you to show how much I care for you?"

Remember, the small cherishing behaviors must not concern past conflicts. Your requests must not be old demands. That is, the requests must not concern any subject over which you have quarreled. To determine a legitimate request, answer the following questions:

1. Can the behaviors be done on an everyday basis?
2. Are the behaviors minor ones—ones that can be changed easily?
3. Are the requests something only your spouse can fulfill? If they are things that a hired hand could perform, the requests may create problems. For example, if they are mostly task-oriented like "Wash the car," "Take out the trash," "Clean out the camper" or "Have the dishes and house all cleaned up by the time I get home," then they do not reflect intimacy and the cultivation of a personal relationship. Some better responses would be, "Ask me what excites me about my new job," "Turn out the lights, and let's sit holding hands without talking" or "Rub my back for five minutes."

If you answered yes to all three questions, then you have a legitimate request. Continue through this process for each request, until your and your spouse's lists include 15 to 18 items. Listing as many as 18 creates more interest and makes it easier for each spouse to follow through with the requests.

Here are more, positive suggestions for your caring lists:

- Say "Hello" to me and kiss me in the morning when we wake up.
- Say "Good-night" to me.
- Bring me home a pretty flower or leaf.
- Call me during the day and ask, "How's it going?"
- Put a candle on the dinner table and turn off the lights.
- Hold me when we're watching TV.
- Leave me a surprise note.
- Take a shower or bath with me when the kids are gone.

- Kiss or touch me when you leave for work.
- Tell me about your best experience during the day.
- Hold my hand in public.
- Tell me I'm nice to be around.
- Praise me in front of the kids.
- Ask me how you can pray for me.

Many of the caring behaviors you request of your spouse may seem unimportant or even trivial. Some may be a bit embarrassing because they appear artificial at first. That is alright. These small behaviors set the tone of a relationship. They are the primary building blocks for a fulfilling marriage. They establish an environment of positive expectations and change negative attitudes.

When your lists are complete, exchange them with each other and discuss the caring behaviors you have requested. Tell your spouse how you would like your requests met. Do not, however, pass judgment on your spouse's requests. Only ask for clarification if needed. Once your discussion is complete, you need to commit to follow through with at least two items from the list each day, whether or not he or she follows through with any positive behaviors on your list.

For example, Ted's wife said, "Ted, remember the way you used to bring me a flower when we were first married? You presented it to me when you met me at the door—after you had kissed me. It made me feel really loved."

During a discussion like this, it is likely that both of you will think of additional cherishing behaviors that you would enjoy receiving. Add them to the lists. The more the better, as long as both lists are approximately equal in length.

The basic principle is this: If couples will increase their positive actions toward each other, they will eventually crowd out and eliminate the negative. Additionally, behaving in a loving, caring way will generate a loving, caring response and will build feelings of love. And yes, this really works. See for yourself.

One therapist used this approach with 200 couples (many of whom went for counseling to help determine whether or not they should divorce). Five years later, 174 of the 200 couples were still married. Of those 174, 89 percent reported a continued high level of commitment to their marriage.[1]

The following concept illustrates the same process in a different way. Take a look. I will call it the relationship bank account.

As is true of a monetary bank account, the balance in the relational bank is in flux because of deposits and withdrawals. Relationship deposits vary in size just like our monetary deposits. The deposits can range in size from a kind word or action to a very large gift of love. Withdrawals also vary. A minor disagreement could be small, but a major offense could drain the account. Zingers are definitely a withdrawal, and so is defensiveness (see chapters 4 and 6).

When you begin thinking of your relationship in this way, you become more aware of deposits and attempted deposits, as well as withdrawals. Naturally, the larger the balance, the healthier the relationship. And just like a monetary account, it is best to have sufficient reserves in your relationship bank account. Unfortunately, many couples live with overdrawn accounts.

You will also find two types of currencies in relationship accounts—his and hers. Each may have a different valuation and may fluctuate from day to day. The difference in this type of bank account is that the "teller," or receiving person, sets the value of a deposit or withdrawal.

If the account has a large balance, a few small withdrawals don't impact the account that much. But if the balance is relatively small or hovers near zero, a small withdrawal definitely impacts the account. The ideal account holder keeps the deposits high and the withdrawals low. And each spouse needs to communicate to the other what he or she perceives as a deposit or a withdrawal. What is a deposit for you? For your spouse? What is a withdrawal for you? For your spouse? It may help you to discuss this concept for clarification.[2]

### Start with Small Steps

Sometimes I find couples who want changes that are reasonable but unattainable at first. Trying for the unattainable right away only breeds discouragement. It is better to work on small, attainable goals. Achieving a number of small steps first will more likely help couples resolve major problems over time. It is better to spend time working on something you can achieve than on something you at first cannot.

An example of this is found in the third step some marriage counselors use to help couples break free from the vicious cycle of reinforcing undesirable behaviors on each other. It is possible to break this cycle on your own, but it takes cooperation from both the husband and wife. It is not a matter of ignoring the behavior but making sure you are not promoting it anymore.

Breaking the cycle involves four steps. The first step is to agree with each other not to become defensive about whatever is written or said. The second step is for each spouse to write out three problem behaviors you both would like to see changed in each other. The problem behaviors should be listed in order of importance. The third step is to list your reactions to each of your spouse's problem behaviors in order to identify how you might reinforce this behavior. The final step is to list desirable, or positive, behaviors you would like to see from your spouse.

The following lists show one wife's response to her husband's problem behaviors:

1. Three of my spouse's problem behaviors I would like to see changed:

   a. He constantly complains about everything.
   b. He forces his ideas, wants and desires on me. He tries to mold me and shape me to conform to his expectations.
   c. He compliments me with qualifications.

2. My reaction to these undesirable behaviors:

   a. His complaining is just the way it is, and he can't do anything about it. Often, I say nothing and just keep it inside.
   b. I am usually hurt by this, and I get angry and try to say something that will hurt him in return. I also tell him that I am sorry that I'm not who he wants me to be.
   c. I respond by usually saying nothing—keeping it inside. Just some kind of recognition would really help.

3. The desirable, or positive, behaviors of my spouse:

   a. He gets excited about something we can both do.
   b. He compliments me in front of other people.
   c. He does the dishes.

Now here is the husband's list in response to his wife's problem behaviors:

1. Three of my spouse's problem behaviors I would like to see changed:

    a. She has no desire for sex. She laughs when kissed and shows no sexual interest at all.
    b. She walks away from me when I am talking to her. She usually tells me to shut up.
    c. She spends the little time we have together picking up things, taking a shower, doing odd jobs, etc.

2. My reaction to these undesirable behaviors:

    a. Kiss her. When I found out that this turned her off, I stopped, trying not to push what obviously annoyed her.
    b. I usually get mad and say things again to make sure she understands.
    c. I usually sit there although sometimes I say something to her. It makes me feel as though her housework is more important than I am.

3. The desirable, or positive, behaviors of my spouse:

    a. She is a good cook.
    b. She works uncomplainingly.
    c. She keeps the house clean.
    d. She is a very good mother to the baby.
    e. She is very organized.
    f. She is dependable.
    g. She is thoughtful about many things.

Once your and your spouse's lists are complete, your next step is quite different from what some would expect. It entails keeping a weekly record of the number of times problem behaviors occur. This log is kept, not to blame or offend each other, but to help each one become aware of his or her own reinforcing response to the behavior.

We begin with the least-threatening behavior because it is easier to work out a mutual agreement with an easier problem. This should help most couples proceed to more serious behaviors, which need elimination over time.

The way to eliminate a problem is to replace your problem behaviors with the desired behaviors your spouse appreciates. If it helps you or your spouse, verbally commit to your spouse that you will no longer respond the way you have. Instead, you will let the problem behavior slide by. This takes patience, commitment and prayer, but it works.[3] What do you have to lose?

## Do the Unexpected

The fourth step brings out positive changes in a relationship by doing the unexpected. This means to do something different when you recognize that what you are doing is just not working. I learned this concept in the early 1960s from a book I read in graduate school. The writer talked about performing the unexpected behavior in relation to raising and disciplining children. Since I was a youth pastor at the time, I wondered if it would work with teenagers, especially in a large meeting setting.

Since most of us are predictable (including me) and continue to respond in the same way, I began to think, *When some kid begins to cut up and create a disturbance, how do I usually react? How do they expect me to respond?* Once I figured that out, I purposefully did something different. Because they weren't expecting it, they couldn't defend against it. I found that it worked. Then as

I moved into counseling couples, I wondered if it would work in marital relationships. I experimented, and it did.

Here are some of the unpredictable things couples have reported doing:

- Instead of telling her husband to calm down and not get angry (which never worked), the wife suggested that he get angry and raise his voice. She pulled two chairs together and said, "Let's sit down and make it easier on ourselves." Interestingly, he calmed down and sat down.
- When a husband occasionally came home late because of traffic, instead of snapping at his wife when she complained that he should have called, he simply said, "Sorry." He then gave her a tape that he had recorded in the car—complete with traffic noise—giving a report every five minutes of where he was and how fast the traffic was moving. There was no argument, and the next time he was late, his wife responded differently.
- Instead of telling her husband that he was yelling again (which he would always deny), a wife turned on a tape recorder in plain view of her husband. This did the trick and the yelling stopped. And the next time he started to yell, as he saw the tape recorder, he stopped yelling.
- On a humorous note, a husband shared with me that he hated being predictable when he came into the house at night, so he thought up different ways of greeting his family when he arrived home. His favorite entry was crawling in the doggy door to surprise everyone.

Yes, you might think some of these behaviors as corny or immature, but they worked. Move beyond yourself and what you are afraid others will think of you, and take the chance that an unpredictable behavior could bring about a much-needed jump start to your marriage.

# CELEBRATE YOUR MARRIAGE

How do you keep positives alive? Celebrate. That is right: Celebrate. Celebration is an important part of a healthy marriage. For example, celebrating a wedding anniversary is a good way for two spouses to signify to each other the value of their relationship. However, a once-a-year celebration is not enough. Try celebrating your marriage vows at least once a month. And it is not necessary to spend a lot of money on these celebrations. Instead, take some time to think and plan an outing, a dinner or just some quiet time together. All celebrations are powerful acts that bond couples together, so observe them faithfully. I have a friend who has celebrated 374 anniversaries!

**Plan an Outing**
Plan an outing for just the two of you at least once a month. Have someone else play with the kids. Don't invite your friends. Remember, gatherings with other people don't count! For some reason, couples have a hard time with this concept. They recite all the things they do in each other's company: attending church and potluck suppers, visiting friends and relatives, going to parties and dinners and cheering their kids at athletic events. They think these outings offer proof of their attempts at togetherness. But think about how much you actually talk to your spouse at these kinds of events. For that matter, how much do you even see your spouse at group gatherings? Let's not even talk about expressions of affection in group settings. Again,

gatherings with other people don't count for these once-a-month outings!

### Take Turns Planning the Event

One month you plan a date, and the next month your spouse plans an outing. Realize that planning and implementing the outing is an important part of expressing your appreciation for your spouse.

### Do Something Your Spouse Would Enjoy

This is a critical point when you plan a celebration. The idea behind monthly celebrations is to give back to your spouse. So when it is your turn to plan a celebration, try to take the attitude, "I am willing to do this for you because I care for you." Participate in the activity cheerfully, not grudgingly. You may even discover that your spouse's interests are worth pursuing yourself or that they are something you can explore together. You may also find that planning activities with your spouse's interests in mind has another unexpected payoff—vicarious pleasure. Joy abounds in seeing another person's joy. If you plan a celebration with the intent of delighting your mate, you will most likely experience a delight of your own.

### Keep Your Celebrations Simple

Your celebrations should be as simple as your time and budget requires. Remember, it is not the gifts or dinner or flowers that count but the time spent together.

### Be Creative

Never repeat an activity more than once a year.

Celebrations work. Why not take an opportunity today to plan a special time with your spouse? The results may surprise you.

# TAKE THE PLUNGE

It is possible for you to change as well as your spouse. However, neither of you can do it alone. God resides in the life of every believer and will help him or her accomplish the desired change. You need to ask yourself, *How can I release the power of God within me? What will help me begin to take risks?* Perhaps Helen's experience will help you sort and answer these questions.

Helen grew more and more frustrated with her husband who was turning into a full-fledged workaholic. Sam was very conscientious about his work, so he was rarely home. To top it off, he had not used any vacation time for three years. Vacations were very important to Helen. She felt that she was raising the children by herself. Her attempts to convey her concern to Sam were met by excuses and promises that if she would just be patient for a few more months, he might be able to cut back. However, to Helen this was an excuse, as he was in a job where he essentially controlled his own time.

Having witnessed the destructive results of this pattern in other families, Helen decided she had to change her approach. Several weeks earlier, she had learned the importance of the suggestions made throughout this chapter. She knew what she had already tried didn't work. There had to be a better way.

Her thought life was positive and hopeful. She began to focus on Scriptures, in particular passages from Proverbs, which dealt with the wisdom of God. These helped her center on how to speak the truth in love (see Eph. 4:15). Helen took a piece of paper and outlined several ideas. Then she began to think of how to apply the Scriptures. After that, she began to visualize what she would try with Sam. Finally, she spent time in prayer asking for wisdom and the courage to act.

One day at work, Sam received a telegram requesting his presence that evening for dinner with "one of his most valuable clients." He was told to arrive at one of the finest restaurants in the city at 6:30 that evening. The telegram stated the importance for him to attend, since he was on the verge of losing this important client. Reservations had been made in his name. The telegram befuddled and perplexed him, and no one he talked to, from fellow workers to secretaries to restaurant personnel, could shed any light on the situation.

However, he decided to go. When he arrived, he was shown to a table and told that the other party would be a few minutes late. A few minutes later, much to his surprise, his wife, Helen, walked in, smiled and sat down. He nearly fell out of his chair.

"Did you send the telegram? Are you the client? What is this?" he asked.

"Yes, I did send the telegram and I am the client," she replied. "I need to talk to you. I feel as though I am one of your neglected clients. Because of the past three years, I've wondered when are you planning to drop me out of your life?"

Sam was shocked. His next few responses were met with the same question, "When are you planning to drop me out of your life, Sam?"

Finally, he said, "What do you mean? I've never planned to drop you, Helen. I care for you. I need you. I love you. I always want you with me."

"But I don't feel that you want me or need me," Helen replied. "I love you, too, and want our marriage to work. But I feel as though I'm a stranger to you. I know your work is important. I appreciate your dedication and diligence. Those are wonderful qualities. However, I want your time, diligence and dedication for our marriage as well. I want to spend this evening with you. So let's go ahead and order dinner, and you can continue to think about what I've said." She opened the menu and then said, "If you would like to talk about how we can build our marriage, I'll listen. But I will not listen to excuses or reasons for not taking action now. I want action and I want you! Let's eat."

Needless to say, Helen did get his attention. Fortunately, her plan worked. In his discussion with her, Sam admitted that her radical approach captured his attention and let him know how serious she was. Not all situations and changes are so radical, but even small changes need the steps that Helen followed.

## Saturate your mind with the image of God's presence.

Visualization, prayer and action—these are the keys. Picture yourself as Helen did, facing some difficult situation with our Lord standing beside you; He takes the first step forward. Then see yourself taking one step forward until you are side by side with Jesus. Saturate your mind with the image of God's presence. This practical visualizing of Scripture in your life can free you from the fear of failure. Sure, it takes time, work and effort. Scripture tells us to gird up our minds (see 1 Pet. 1:13). It's worth a try! There has to be a better way! And there is! Now, it's your choice.

## TAKE-AWAY QUESTIONS

If you could change your marriage, what would you do differently? Answer the following questions to identify how you can change your marriage for the better:

1. Think of an issue you would identify as a problem in your marriage and describe it.

2. When doesn't this problem happen?

3. What is different about this time?

4. How do you think differently?

5. If you woke tomorrow with this problem solved, what would you be doing differently?

For any additional problems identified in your marriage, answer the five questions pertaining to those problems on a separate piece of paper. You'll be surprised at the difference this makes.

To determine your willingness to change and your commitment level when making a change, circle the word that best completes each statement.

1. I am willing to make **any, most, some, minor, very few** changes or adjustments necessary to improve our marriage together.

2. I believe my spouse is willing to make **any, most, some, minor, very few** changes or adjustments necessary to improve our marriage together.

3. It is **very important, somewhat important, not very important** to me that my spouse is satisfied and fulfilled.

4. My commitment level to improving my marriage is

| Little or none | | | | Average | | | | Absolute | | |
|---|---|---|---|---|---|---|---|---|---|---|
| 0 | 1 | 2 | 3 | 4 | 5 | 6 | 7 | 8 | 9 | 10 |

5. My spouse's commitment level to improving our marriage is

| Little or none | | | | Average | | | | Absolute | | |
|---|---|---|---|---|---|---|---|---|---|---|
| 0 | 1 | 2 | 3 | 4 | 5 | 6 | 7 | 8 | 9 | 10 |

Finally, answer the following questions:

1. What personal and marital behaviors would you like to change in yourself?

2. What personal and marital behaviors would you like to see changed in your spouse?

3. What personal and marital behaviors would your spouse like to see changed in you?

4. Describe in specific detail which of the methods in this chapter you will implement during the week.

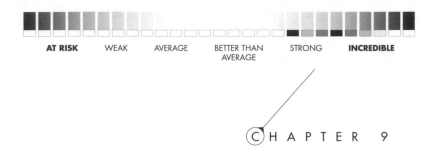

# CHAPTER 9

# Vows—New and Old

Remember that special day? You stood facing each other and recited your marriage vows. Your marital history began on that day. Do you remember what you said at that time? If so, what do those vows mean to you at this point in your marriage?

How can you continue to fulfill the commitment you made on your wedding day? *Grace.* God's grace is the only way a couple can survive all the pressures and temptations today. Answering and discussing the questions in this book, creating a plan of action and even starting to celebrate once a month can bring a fresh start to any marriage. However, if couples do not include God and His grace in whatever method they choose, their marriage vows will be difficult to fulfill. Mike Mason in *The Mystery of Marriage* sums up this truth:

There are no lasting marriages without the continuing secret touch of His grace, which comes to a couple in the form of the uncanny ability to keep a set of highly improbable promises to one another, promises involving such normally evanescent qualities as love, honor, trust, faithfulness.[1]

# REFLECT ON THE MEANING OF YOUR VOWS

What words did you express in your wedding vows to your life-long friend? What do those words mean to you? Very few couples ever sit down and explain to each other what they meant by their vows. They just assume that their spouse understands what the sacred words mean. Perhaps now would be a good time to explain to each other what you meant when you promised to respect, to be faithful and to be friends. Think about some of these words.

### Respect

Is there respect in your marriage? Respect in marriage means ministering to your spouse through listening, a loving embrace, a flexible mind and attitude and a gracious spirit. It means looking past faults and differences and seeing strengths and similarities. It means mutually sharing concerns instead of attempting to carry the load yourself.

Perhaps these questions will help as you evaluate your respect for one another:

- In a tense situation, do I cut off my spouse when he or she holds a different view from mine?
- When I think my spouse is wrong, do I become offensive and harsh, and try to put him or her in place?

- In trying to get a point across, am I gently persuasive or opinionated and demanding?
- Am I driven so much by the need to be right that I try to pressure my spouse into my position? Do I intimidate my spouse?

It is true, these are meddling questions, but answering them is a good step toward building a respectful marriage. As the author Judith Lechman said, respect begins when we "learn to practice careful listening rather than threatened opposition, honest expression rather than resentment, flexibility rather than rigidity, loving censure rather than harsh coercion, encouragement rather than intimidation."[2]

### Faithfulness

Most people think of faithfulness in sexual terms—"I'm faithful because I'm not sleeping around." But exceptional couples have a broader understanding of this word. To them, faithfulness, the promise to "forsake all others," includes all friendships, family-of-origin commitments, career opportunities and community

## Love increases in marriage when spouses are friends.

involvement that do not serve to increase love. We are faithful in marriage when we keep the promises we made in the past, similar to how God's Word tells us we are faithful when we keep His commandments. How do you express faithfulness? How do you describe faithfulness? Think about how faithfulness is expressed in either the physical and mental health of you and your spouse or in the intimacy of your marriage.

## Friendship

Love increases in marriage when spouses are friends. Sometimes this is called companionship, or "companioning." Ron Hawkins provides some helpful thoughts on this subject in his book *Marital Intimacy*:

- Good companioning involves our free choice of our partner as a companion and our unconditional acceptance of his or her unique personality.
- Good companioning requires a commitment to major ing on the positive while in the presence of the companion.
- Good companioning involves our free choice to spend the bulk of leisure time with the companion of choice.
- Good companioning results from our willingness to allow for and support individual differences. Good companions don't try to make each other over to fit some predetermined mold.
- Good companioning involves a willingness to speak to a partner in a language of love that communicates.
- Good companions do not try to meet every need that partners have. We meet those we have the resources to meet. Only Jesus Christ can meet some of our mate's needs.[3]

Hawkins also expresses companionship in the form of gifts:

- Spend time together. We give the gift of time.
- Have fun together. We give the gift of laughter.

- Share feelings and thoughts. We give the gift of sharing.
- Like being together. We give the gift of appreciation.
- Discuss issues. We give the gift of confidence.
- Survive crises together. We give the gift of dependability.
- Discuss fears. We give the gift of vulnerability.
- Cover our partner's weaknesses. We give the gift of protection.
- Celebrate our individual values together. We give the gift of respect.
- Encourage a life separate from our life together. We give the gift of separateness.
- Speak the truth together. We give the gift of honesty.
- Handle conflict together. We give the gift of surfaced anger.
- Practice forgiveness. We give the gift of forgiveness.
- Practice unconditional acceptance. We give the gift of love.[4]

How is friendship in your marriage?

## RECOGNIZE THAT VOWS EQUAL COMMITMENT

When you married, you pledged to keep your wedding vows. Jesus challenged you not to let anyone or anything come between you and your spouse that would cause you to break your vows. How are marital vows kept? By your own strength? Not so. Mike Mason states that, "The marriage vows give glory to God. While it is true that a man and a woman on their wedding day take a step toward a unique fulfillment of the commandment of love, it is even more true to say of matrimony that it is a sacramental outpouring of God's grace enabling such love to take place.[5] Again, we are reminded of the sustaining grace of God.

Does the word "commitment" come to mind when you reflect on your wedding vows?

The word "commitment" is not used in the Bible, but its derivatives "committed" and "commit" are used in the Bible. Commitment can be thought of as both doing or practicing something and delivering or entrusting something to a person. Commitment involves the binding or pledging of oneself to a particular course of action. It also implies a choice based on reasoning. The act of entrusting oneself to another should be supported by sound reasoning. Man and woman should be able to provide rational arguments for why their marriage is healthy and why it should be expected to flourish.

## Commitment implies a pledge by each spouse to fidelity for life.

Commitment implies a pledge by each spouse to fidelity for life. When commitment is present, a couple enters into an irrevocable covenant. They pledge their faithfulness, regardless of circumstances. It reminds me of the spirit of Hernando Cortez, when in 1519, he landed his troops at Vera Cruz, Mexico. The more than 6,000 men were irrevocably committed to their task of conquering the new land for the mother country. When Cortez set fire to the vessels that brought them, the men could not retreat. As this example shows, commitment is not something you can turn away from.

## The 50/50 Relationship

Often when two people get married, they have expectations of how the relationship should work. The unspoken assumption is that "my spouse will meet me halfway." Sometimes this is called the 50/50 Plan.

The 50/50 Plan says "You do your part, and I'll do mine." It sounds logical, but couples who think it works may be surprised. Read the following example of a 50/50 relationship:

A young man saw an elderly couple sitting down to lunch at McDonald's. He noticed that they had ordered one meal and an extra drink cup. As he watched, the gentleman carefully divided the hamburger in half and then counted out the fries, one for him, one for her, until each had half of them. Then he poured half of the soft drink into the extra cup and set that in front of his wife. The old man then began to eat, and his wife sat watching, with her hands folded in her lap. The young man decided to ask if they would allow him to purchase another meal for them so that they didn't have to split their meal.

The old gentleman said, "Oh no. We've been married for 50 years, and everything has always been and will be shared 50/50."

The young man then asked the wife if she was going to eat, and she replied, "Not yet. It's his turn with the teeth."

You see, the problem with most 50/50 arrangements is that giving is based on merit and performance. A focus exists more on what the other person is giving than on what we are giving. And who are you to judge if your spouse has met you halfway?

## The 100/100 Relationship

There is a better plan—the 100/100 Plan. The idea is to give 100 percent, no matter what your spouse does. It really does work!

In a 100/100 relationship, commitment is the unconditional acceptance of the other spouse. It is the surrender of personal pleasure and comfort.

Commitment does cost, because dependability has a price tag. However, in return you will receive an encouraging spouse who gives the gift of sympathetic understanding and says no to personal desires, which cuts back selfish desires. Commitment also means organizing one's time, thoughts and resources for the benefit of others. It means the surrender of a measure of personal freedom and rights.[6]

Imagine for a moment that your wedding to your spouse is taking place today. If you were to rewrite your wedding vows now, what would you commit to and promise to do in order to establish an unconditional relationship? Before you think of your own answers, consider the answers from other couples:

- "My commitment to you is to listen to your concerns each day for the purpose of having the kind of marriage we both want."
- "I realize that our love will change. I will work to maintain a high level of romance, courtship and love in our relationship."
- "I pledge to confront problems when they arise and not retreat like a turtle into my shell."
- "I commit myself to you in times of joy and in times of problems. We will tackle and share our problems together."
- "I promise that I will never be too busy to look at the flowers with you."

- "I will respect your beliefs and capabilities that are different from mine. I will not attempt to make you into a revised edition of me."
- "I will be open and honest with no secrets, and I desire you to be the same with me."
- "I will reflect God's Word in my relationship with you."

Which of these would you select for your marriage? Or create your own.

## RENEW YOUR VOWS

More and more couples are having reaffirmation ceremonies. Why? Because it is a positive step for a couple. The ceremony signifies a continued commitment.

Someone once said that if the wedding ceremony is the celebration of falling in love and starting a marriage, a reaffirmation ceremony could be considered the celebration of still being in love and staying married.

I've participated in several of these events. One was the ceremony of a close friend and his wife. They married in high school, had a baby right away and at first lived in a converted chicken coop while working on an egg farm. They met the Lord a few years later, which changed their lives. They wanted to declare their lasting commitment to each other and to Jesus Christ at a reaffirmation ceremony. It was a special time, not just for them, but for all their loved ones.

Another couple I knew had been separated for almost two years. The husband became involved with someone else during that time, but fortunately that relationship dissolved. A few months later he became a Christian in a very dramatic, life-changing way. Then he and his wife reunited. They decided to have a reaffirmation ceremony in their backyard. They created new, meaningful vows and recited them. At the ceremony, they also shared with everyone their personal journey and gave an invitation to accept the Lord. It was a very moving and powerful time.

Some of you may have read the two examples given above but are still wondering why couples renew their vows. Well, it is not done for couples to meet any of society's standards, legal requirements or religious guidelines. It is done simply because the couples want to.

Read the following excerpt from the book *Reaffirmation*. The excerpt highlights the purpose behind a reaffirmation ceremony.

It's a chance to redefine their marriage, rededicate themselves, celebrate what they've accomplished and look ahead to what they have before them. Though that personal statement may include many of the elements of a first-time wedding, the emphasis is very much on their own relationship and commitment, on all the unique and personal things that have made their marriage endure.

In reaffirmation all the forms and customs of wedding take on a special meaning. While many first weddings are events involving the families of the bride and groom, a reaffirmation celebrates the family you've created together. A reaffirmation is given by you, not by your parents, you are the hosts, and your parents are honored guests who share your day with you. A reaffirmation is also a chance to include your children in your marriage in a very meaningful way. It's their chance to do something for you through their presence and participation in your event. A reaffirmation can be very much a reflection of your family history—the roots of

your marriage, your experience through the years, your
hopes for the future.[7]

In a sense, reaffirming vows is the opposite of a divorce
decree. It is an act of rejoicing over the fact that you have made
marriage work, made marriage fulfilling and weathered the
storms. Reaffirmation is the outward public demonstration of
renewing your commitment to one another. It is outward
because it takes daily effort and commitment for your marriage
to be all you want it to be.

Reaffirmation, like renewing, is once again making a choice—
a new choice. The reasons for this act are probably much different from the reasons you originally intended on your wedding
day. Instead of an act based on the hope of future dreams fulfilled, it is an act based upon your history, as well as a continued
hope for the future. Marriage therapist Dave Viscott describes
reaffirmation this way:

> Reaffirmation is, first of all, an exploration, a redefini-
> tion of where you are as a couple. It can involve a ques-
> tioning of the whole marital relationship. Each partner
> may ask, "Am I getting what I want or need out of this
> relationship? What if my spouse gets really sick and
> becomes bedridden or infirm—how will I feel about
> taking care of him or her? Will I be overwhelmed by
> resentment and bitterness—granted that everyone has
> some resentment and still remains a person who cares
> for his or her spouse? Have we as a couple continued to
> develop interests in common, or has our life together
> become boring and repetitive? Do we stimulate each
> other intellectually? And how important is that aspect
> of our lives? The years of my life are precious ones.

Do I trust my mate enough to risk spending them with him or her?"

Reaffirmation challenges me to examine myself, as well. "Where am I at this point in my life? Where do I want to go? Has my relationship enabled me to grow sufficiently, or have I found it to be thwarting and confining? When we first met, we married for very specific reasons. Are those reasons still valid? Have they changed? If I were to marry again now, would I select the same mate?"

Deciding to renew your vows can involve some soul-searching questions. It takes people who have a good sense of who they are and who have sufficient self-esteem to be able to take a long, hard, honest look at themselves and their relationship. But questions needn't be frightening. They have the potential for leading you to a place that's deeper, richer, more profound.[8]

How can an affirmation service be a memorable experience, not only for you, but for those in attendance? While this service is for you and your marriage, it also presents an opportunity to minister to others. Here are some ideas for what your reaffirmation ceremony could include:

- If you videotaped your wedding, select portions of it to play at the beginning of the reaffirmation ceremony or throughout the service. Or pictures can be made into a video scrapbook.
- If you have taken videos over the course of your marriage, show brief segments and then describe what was going on in your life at that time. If this is your 25th anniversary, show pictures or film in 5-year increments.

If it's a 50th anniversary, select photos in 10-year increments.

- One or both of you could share what you have learned
  during your marriage. This could be done live or videotaped beforehand.
- You may want to share significant quotes from books
  on marriage that you've read.
- You may want to reaffirm your vows in a private ceremony with no one in attendance. You could have it
  videotaped and then send copies to significant people
  in your life.
- Tell those in attendance what you'll need from them
  for the future enhancement of your marriage. Give people the opportunity to share with you and the group
  words of wisdom, encouragement or blessing.
- If your parents are living, you might want to include
  them in the ceremony.

A reaffirmation ceremony is your celebration, so plan whatever you like. (After all, you'll likely be footing the bill.) Perhaps
you will not only want your children in attendance but involved
in the planning as well. For example, some senior couples
involve grandchildren as well as great-grandchildren. But
remember, this is your occasion, so don't feel you have to invite
relatives—or anyone for that matter—out of a sense of obliga-
tion. This event needs to represent your thoughts, feelings,
needs and desires—from the invitation sent (if any) to the location you choose. The friends you invite may be some of those
who came to your wedding, as well as new ones. And when you
begin to create your renewal vows, feel free to elaborate on the
sample vows that appear later in this chapter. Again, the ceremony is up to you. It can be serious, funny, formal or casual.

The bottom line is to have fun and remind each other of your commitment to one another.

## CREATE RENEWAL VOWS

How do you fashion vows of reaffirmation? This is a time of realistic recommitment. It is also a time to reflect back over the history of your marriage and perhaps incorporate some of those experiences into your vows. And for some, this may mean lengthy vows. For others, maybe not. For some, it's easy to speak off-the-cuff and remember everything you want to say. For others, it is not. For some, memorizing a lengthy selection is quite easy, but for others it is a pressurized chore. When creating your vows, do not worry about the presentation details. Instead, focus on making the day as relaxed and as comfortable as you can. You may want to reflect on the following topics when creating your vows. I promise that they will enrich your vows.

- When or where you met
- Your first impressions
- What drew you to your spouse
- When you first realized you were in love
- Your first kiss
- Your favorite places
- Reasons why you married this person
- Reasons why you're glad you married this person
- Dreams for marriage you had that were realized
- Surprises you've experienced in your marriage
- Special times you experienced when dating and during marriage
- Special anniversaries and celebrations
- A time when you especially experienced God's presence together

## Sample Renewal Vows

Read through the sample vows provided to aid you and your spouse in creating your very own, unique vows.

*Husband:* I am standing before you now, much calmer and more aware of what I am doing than I was the day we joined together. You have become my best friend, my favorite person, my lover, my spouse in parenting. I hold you tighter now than ever before, because I am so much more aware of what I would lose if you were not with me. As we renew our vows, I am much more aware of what I am saying and doing than I was many years ago. I am glad to do this over again. What you and I have been through together God has used to shape us into who He wants us to become. There have been difficult times, differences and challenges. We have learned to cook and eat new dishes, and adjust to our different families. I would never trade any of these experiences, because we were together in all of them.

When I was weak, you were strong. When I had a need, you were there. You encouraged me and believed in me. I commit my self, heart and mind to you, and you can count on me for the rest of our days. I loved you first as a girlfriend, then as a fiancée, next as a bride and now as my lifelong companion. I thank God for you and will pray for you each day.

*Wife:* I stand here today holding your hands tightly. I didn't want you to ever get away the first time I saw you, and I still don't. That's why I am recommitting myself to you today and forever. You have changed as I have changed. You are more confident, still thoughtful and choose your words carefully. Even though your words are not as abundant as mine, I delight in hearing every one, and I am willing to wait for them. We both have changed physically. A bit of gray dots the side of your head, and I love the color. Wrinkles are beginning and will become more pronounced. If you can stand mine, I know I will love yours. Thank you for your commitment over the years, which I saw in changing diapers, tolerating my new recipes, asking first if I was alright when you saw the dented fender and helping me when I cried, rather than trying to fix me. Thank you for believing in me. I look forward to being by your side, being in your bed, being in the boat on the lake and helping you gather the money we'll need for our children's weddings and then for our grandchildren.

I commit myself to always being your bride, in sickness or in health, when finances are abundant or when the bills have stacked up. I will continue to learn who you are as you continue to learn who I am. And I will continue to bring you before our Lord and Savior, Jesus, each day of our lives.

What are the vows that you want for your marriage at this time? What vows do you think your spouse wants at this time?

## TAKE-AWAY QUESTIONS

Let's start with an exercise that takes you back in time. Write your own marriage story, and as you do so, use the following questions to help you. Your history can be an excellent teacher. While you can't rewrite or edit portions of your marriage story that are in the past, you can write the chapters that have yet to be written. The future is up to you. Allow this assessment experience to help you write the chapters in a positive way. Additionally, use it as a tool to help you create your renewal vows.

Remember your courtship:

1. Where did you meet?

2. What attracted you to your spouse?

3. What did you think of your spouse the first time you kissed?

4. What were four reasons why you married your spouse?

5. When you decided to marry your spouse, who was the first person you told and what was that person's response?

6. What were two of the most positive experiences during your first year of marriage?

7. What was the dream you had for your marriage?

8. As best you can remember, what were your wedding
   vows?

Did you remember your wedding vows? Did you recall the
specifics? What were they? What did you commit yourself to for
the rest of your life? Since most of us don't remember, how can we
follow through and live up to those commitments? Why not consider a reaffirmation ceremony for your marriage? It will help you
to remember the faithful promises once pledged, and it could be
a life-changing experience. By having this ceremony, you and your
spouse can say to all, "We've made it for 25 (or 50) years, and we
want to renew the step we took ages ago."

Stop and reflect:

1. What feelings emerged from these questions?

2. What feelings emerged from your spouse as he or she
   listened to your answers?

3. When was the last time you and your spouse shared these questions and answers?

4. Why not renew your vows today?

# Final Thoughts

Take a moment and think back to the day you picked up *The Marriage Checkup*. More specifically, think back to when you began scoring yourself on the level of satisfaction and level of communication surveys. Were you surprised at your and your spouse's scores? Or were your scores expected? From that point on, you immersed yourself in various marital issues, ranging from love languages to sinful thoughts to forgiveness to methods of success. You were provided opportunities to reflect on your relationship and answer detailed questions pertaining to the various discussion-based topics. What did you find out?

It is my hope and prayer that God revealed to you and your spouse how you could move your marriage from where it currently stands to where you want it to go. And it is with a sense of urgency that I encourage you to take what God has told you and move forward with a plan of action. Why now? Because life is too short.

Life is fragile. So is marriage. We have learned that lesson, oh so well, since September 11, 2001. That is when our lives changed. Couples said good-bye to one another that morning as they had done for years. For some, it was a casual remark; for others, it was said with passion and meaning. Some made dates to meet for dinner or for an evening out. For many, the dates were never realized.

Who would have known that by 9:30 that morning there would be hundreds of widows and widowers sitting in shock and dismay?

A few were able to make a final call to their loved ones. Some called from the towers to say good-bye; others called from the planes to say the same. During the next few days and weeks, spouses listened to the last messages on their answering machines or continued to check cell phones with the hope of new messages. Phone companies received calls from husbands and wives asking if they could check the records to see if any calls had been made on their spouse's cell phone. In most cases, there were no records of any calls.

One couple's story started with their typical commute into work. Each morning, they followed a predictable itinerary—ride the subway together to a stop near Wall Street, walk to the front door of her building, part with a kiss and possible plans for lunch, wait for 15 minutes until he reached his office high in the World Trade Center and then wave out their windows to each other during a "Have a great day!" phone call. But what happened differently on the morning of September 11 was that a plane struck near his window during their phone call. There were no more calls after that sad day.

All of us as couples have crises to face in a day-to-day manner. In one way or another, we may have our own personal September 11 tragedy.

Let me share with you the story of my very close friend's marriage. Dale was 53 and his wife was 40 when they met. He had waited many years to find the "right one," so for this day to come was an answer to prayer. He told me that he wouldn't marry a woman with children, since he'd never had any; and being in his 50s, he didn't know if he could handle step-children. But the Lord had other plans, since the woman he met had children, ages 21, 18 and 9! This is his story, and he has a message for you:

> My wife and I met through the Internet, but really it was through a lot of prayer. God just used that to allow us to find each other. We both had been looking a long time for the right person but never seemed to find the "right one." That was until I got an e-mail from a nurse in San Diego, asking me to write her because she thought we might have a number of things in common. I did, and I could tell from her correspondence that her heart was very sincere and that I found a very special lady. After writing and talking on the phone for what seemed like weeks, we met in Julian, where she was on a church retreat for the weekend. She proceeded to tell me as we walked and talked that at the retreat while praying, Jesus had told her that I was going to marry her. I looked at her a little surprised and told her that He hadn't told me that—and she asked me—"Have you asked Him?"
>
> We had such a great first date that we decided to get together again the next day and go for a walk on the beach; she took me to her favorite beach—Del Mar. After walking for a while on the beach, she told me that she wanted to show me around other parts of Del Mar, so we continued to walk. We went past beautiful parks, art galleries, food places—then we came to this beautiful church and walked around looking at the stained glass, where she then told me, "I would love to get married someday in this church." Not realizing that this was the church that she already attended and had so many friends at,

I told her, "That's nice." Well, six months later we were married and married in that church—and yes, Jesus did tell me that she was the one.

Dale and Sherry expected to be married for many years after exchanging their wedding vows. Neither expected her to develop lung cancer. Dale's story continues:

From the time Sherry and I first knew that she had cancer, she knew she was in a battle for her life, but she also felt that she was in a win-win situation. If she lived, she would be able to continue to have a wonderful life here on Earth; and if she didn't, she would be in heaven with her Lord. But she really wanted to live with her family. She loved being married, loved me so deeply and wanted to beat this terrible disease so badly that she underwent chemotherapy, did all kinds of holistic medicines, acupuncture and even had a special machine that she would use for one hour every night that had good results on other types of cancer. She spent a long time daily with God asking Him to heal her if it was His will, but God had other plans for her.

What Sherry and I had in the three and a half years together was packed with so many memories. We thought we were making up for things we missed out on in the past, but we didn't realize we were doing things for the future we wouldn't have together. We had a wonderful time and life together, and neither of us would have changed it for anything, and I would do it over again in a second if God gave me that chance. If there would be one thing from this that could be passed on to any couple, it would be to enjoy every minute you have together . . . as it could be your last.

As you reflect on Dale and Sherry's story, remember these precious points:

- Don't take one another for granted.
- Don't take your marriage for granted.
- Each moment is precious, so redeem the time.

So why wait on your plan of action for your marriage? The time is now, and God will lead you to a better place if you open your eyes to see and your ears to hear.

## TAKE-AWAY QUESTIONS

1. List three marital goals you have for the next year.

2. List three marital goals you have for the next five years.

# Epilogue

After counseling couples for 35 years, I've reached several conclusions. First, many couples do not need the expense of a counselor (myself or anyone else!) if

- they put into practice what they already know;
- they read some of the books available and put what they read into practice;
- they quit focusing on changing their spouse and make their own changes (you can change your marriage by yourself);
- they use the energy they put into blame and focusing on what isn't working, and turn it into accepting responsibility for and identifying what is working;
- they become focused on hope;
- they answer the question, If what you're doing isn't working, why keep doing it? and make a course correction;
- they apply the following Scriptures to their attitude toward their marriage and spouse:

Finally, brethren, whatever is true, whatever is honorable, whatever is right, whatever is pure, whatever is lovely, whatever is of good repute, if there is any excellence and if anything worthy of praise, let your mind dwell on these things (Phil. 4:8, *NASB*).

Love bears up under anything and everything that comes, is ever ready to believe the best of every person, its hopes are fadeless under all circumstances, and it endures everything [without weakening] (1 Cor. 13:7, *AMP*).

Let all bitterness and indignation and wrath (passion, rage, bad temper) and resentment (anger, animosity) and quarreling (brawling, clamor, contention) and slander (evil-speaking, abusive or blasphemous language) be banished from you, with all malice (spite, ill will, or baseness of any kind). And become useful and helpful and kind to one another, tenderhearted (compassionate, understanding, loving-hearted), forgiving one another [readily and freely], as God in Christ forgave you (Eph. 4:31-32, *AMP*).

Where do you go from here? What do you do with the part of your marriage story that is yet to be written? And yes, you do have a lot of influence on how it unfolds. Your first stop is prayer. Do not attempt to write the remaining chapters in your marriage story by yourself. Instead, gain creativity from Jesus Christ, who guides, instructs, encourages and empowers you. He wants your marriage to be all you want it to be and more. He desires your fulfillment so that you will reflect His presence.

Next, you must continue to grow and make your marriage a priority by seeking information and guidance from books, study guides and, perhaps, counseling. Whether you were encouraged or discouraged by your satisfaction- and communication-level scores, and the many other questions throughout this book, be sure to tap in to the following resources:

To improve your communication, read the following:

> *Communication: Key to Your Marriage* by H. Norman Wright (Regal Books)

To improve your spiritual relationship, read the following:

> *Experiencing God Together* by Dr. Dave Stoop (Tyndale House)
> *Quiet Times for Couples* by H. Norman Wright (Harvest House)
> *After You Say I Do Devotional* by H. Norman Wright (Harvest House)

To improve your sexual relationship, read the following:

> *Men and Sex* by Cliff and Joyce Penner (Thomas Nelson)
> *Celebration of Sex* by Doug Rosenau (Thomas Nelson)

To find out in even greater detail where you and your spouse stand on marital issues such as finances, decision-making, communication, etc., read and respond to the following inventory:

> *The Marriage Checkup Questionnaire* by H. Norman Wright (Regal Books)

If you are in a stepfamily and have been struggling, listen to the following complete seminar on audiocassette:

*Building a Successful Step Family* by Ron Deal. This resource has changed many stepfamilies.

If you have been feeling that your marriage is over or you are considering divorce, please do the following before you make a final decision:

Listen to the tape series *Love Life* by Dr. Ed Wheat.
Watch the video series *Before You Divorce*.
Seek professional help.

To obtain any of these resources, please contact Christian Marriage Enrichment at (800) 875-7560, or your local Christian bookstore.

## TAKE-AWAY QUESTIONS

1. What books have you read on marriage and what nuggets of truth have you mined from them?

2. What books has your spouse read on marriage and what truths has he or she shared with you?

3. What marriage enrichment conferences have you and your spouse attended and what did you decide to work on as a result of the teaching and reflection time?

# Endnotes

## Chapter 1

1. H. Norman Wright, *The Marriage Checkup Questionnaire* (Ventura, CA: Regal Books, 2002).

## Chapter 3

1. Stu Weber, *Tender Warrior: God's Intention for a Man* (Portland, OR: Multnomah Press, 1994), n.p.
2. Gary Chapman, *The Five Love Languages: How to Express Heartfelt Commitment to Your Mate* (Chicago: Northfield Publications, 1992), n.p.
3. Gregory K. Popcak, *The Exceptional Seven Percent: The Nine Secrets of the World's Happiest Couples* (New York: Citadel Press, 2000), n.p.
4. Jerry Richardson and Joel Margulis, *Magic of Rapport* (San Francisco: Harper Publications, 1981); Robert Dilts, *Applications of Neuro-Linguistic Programming* (Cupertino, CA: Meta Publications, 1983); Tracy Cabot, *How to Keep a Man in Love with You Forever* (New York: McGraw-Hill, 1986).
5. Cabot, *How to Keep a Man in Love with You Forever*, pp. 111-113 (see footnote 4 above).

## Chapter 4

1. Dr. Richard Matteson and Janis Long Harris, *What If I Married the Wrong Person?* (Minneapolis, MN: Bethany House, 1996), pp. 234-235.
2. Clifford I. Notorius and Howard J. Markman, *We Can Work It Out: How to Solve Conflicts, Save Your Marriage, and Strengthen Your Love for Each Other* (New York: GP Putnam's Sons, 1993), pp. 20-21.
3. Ibid., p. 27.
4. Ibid., p. 28.
5. Ibid.
6. Ed and Carol Neuenschwander, *Two Friends in Love: Growing Together in Marriage* (Portland, OR: Multnomah Press, 1986), p. 108.
7. David Keirsey and Marilyn Bates, *Please Understand Me: Character and Temperament Types* (Del Mar, CA: Prometheus Nemesis Books, 1978), p. 1.
8. Notorius and Markman, *We Can Work It Out*, p. 33.
9. Ibid.

## Chapter 5

1. Paul W. Coleman, *The Forgiving Marriage: Resolving Anger and Resentment and Rediscovering Each Other* (Chicago: Contemporary Books, 1989), pp. 47-52.

2. *Merriam-Webster's Collegiate Dictionary*, 10th ed., s.v. "slander."
3. Clifford I. Notorius and Howard J. Markman, *We Can Work It Out: How to Solve Conflicts, Save Your Marriage, and Strengthen Your Love for Each Other* (New York: GP Putnam's Sons, 1993), p. 139.
4. Ibid., pp. 144-145.
5. Steven Covey, *The Seven Habits of Highly Effective People* (New York: Simon and Schuster, 1989), pp. 30-31.
6. Alan Loy McGinnis, *Bringing Out the Best in People: How to Enjoy Helping Others Excel* (Minneapolis, MN: Augsburg Press, 1985), p. 100.
7. John M. Gottman and Nan Silver, *Why Marriages Succeed or Fail* (New York: Simon and Schuster, 1994), pp. 182-183.
8. Margaret Davison Campolo, "Reflecting Each Other," in *Husbands and Wives*, eds. Howard and Jeanne Hendricks (Wheaton, IL: Victor Books, 1988), pp. 284-285.

## Chapter 6

1. John M. Gottman and Nan Silver, *Why Marriages Succeed or Fail* (New York: Simon and Schuster, 1994), pp. 56-57.
2. Ibid., pp. 70-102.
3. Clifford I. Notorius and Howard J. Markman, *We Can Work It Out: How to Solve Conflicts, Save Your Marriage, and Strengthen Your Love for Each Other* (New York: GP Putnam's Sons, 1993), pp. 123-124.
4. Manuel Smith, *When I Say No, I Feel Guilty* (New York: Bantam Books, 1985), p. 104.

## Chapter 7

1. Lewis B. Smedes, "Forgiveness: The Power to Change the Past," *Christianity Today* (January 7, 1983), p. 26.
2. William Hendrickson, *New Testament Commentary, Exposition of Ephesians* (Grand Rapids, MI: Baker Book House, 1967), pp. 223-224.
3. Dennis and Matthew Linn, *Healing of Memories* (Ramsey, NJ: Paulist Press, 1974), pp. 94-96; Dennis and Matthew Linn, *Healing Life's Hurts* (Ramsey, NJ: Paulist Press, 1977), p. 218ff; Howard Halpern, *Cutting Loose: An Adult's Guide to Coming to Terms with Your Parents* (New York: Bantam, 1978), p. 212ff; David L. Luecke, *The Relationship Manual* (Columbia, MD: Relationship Institute, 1981), pp. 88-91.
4. Paul W. Coleman, *The Forgiving Marriage: Resolving Anger and Resentment and Rediscovering Each Other* (Chicago: Contemporary Books, 1989), pp. 22-23.
5. Lewis B. Smedes, *Forgive and Forget: Healing the Hurts We Don't Deserve* (San Francisco: Harper and Row, Publishers, Inc., 1984), p. 37.

## Chapter 8

1. Richard B. Stuart, "An Operant Interpersonal Program for Couples," quoted in Daniel Olson, *Treating Relationships* (Lake Mills, IA: Graphic Publishing Company Inc., 1976), p. 130.
2. Clifford I. Notorius and Howard J. Markman, *We Can Work It Out: How to Solve Conflicts, Save Your Marriage, and Strengthen Your Love for Each Other* (New York: GP Putnam's Sons, 1993), pp. 70-73.
3. Alan F. Rappaport and Janet E. Harrel, "A Behavioral Exchange Model for Marital Counseling," quoted in Alan S. Gurman and David G. Rice, *Couples in Conflict* (New York: Jason Aronson, Inc., 1975), pp. 268-269.


## Chapter 9

1. Mike Mason, *The Mystery of Marriage* (Portland, OR: Multnomah Publishers, Inc., 2001), p. 92.
2. Judith C. Lechman, "Love as Respect," in *Husbands and Wives*, eds. Howard and Jeanne Hendricks (Wheaton, IL: Victor Books, 1988), pp. 46-47.
3. Ronald E. Hawkins, *Marital Intimacy* (Grand Rapids, MI: Baker Book House, 1991), pp. 135-137.
4. Ibid.
5. Mason, *The Mystery of Marriage*, p. 97.
6. Hawkins, *Marital Intimacy*, pp. 35-36.
7. Susan Lane, Sandra Carter and Ann Scharffenberger, *Reaffirmation* (New York: Harmony Books, 1982), p. 14.
8. Dave Viscott, *I Love You, Let's Work It Out* (New York: Simon and Schuster, 1987), pp. 279-281, 283-284.